STÉPHANE MALLARMÉ: POEMS

THE NEW CLASSICS SERIES

STÉPHANE *Mallarmé*

Poems

TRANSLATED BY ROGER FRY

WITH COMMENTARIES BY CHARLES MAURON

THE NEW CLASSICS SERIES

The Publisher expresses his thanks to Mlle. Suzanne Antony for assistance in proofreading the French texts in this volume

MANUFACTURED IN THE UNITED STATES
BY THE VAIL-BALLOU PRESS, INC., BINGHAMTON, N. Y.

New Directions Books are published by James Laughlin

NEW YORK OFFICE—333 SIXTH AVENUE—14

Typographic Design by Maurice Serle Kaplan

Jacket Design by Alvin Lustig

THE ORDER of the contents in this volume would be very
mystifying to scholars without the following explanation: It was the first purpose of this New Classics edition to restore to print Roger Fry's excellent translations
of some of Mallarmé's poems (originally published in
London in 1936 by Messers Chatto & Windus) and
the perceptive commentaries of his French friend and
collaborator Charles Mauron. Thanks to the kindness
of Monsieur Mauron, the original publishers and of
Mr Fry's sister it was possible to make the necessary
copyright arrangements. But, alas, Roger Fry had only
lived to translate 29 out of the 64 poems which make
up the canon of Mallarmé's *Poésies* in the standard
French editions. Therefore, in order to make this edition
more useful for students, it seemed advisable to add the
French texts, at least, of the poems not translated.
This has been done in the section beginning on page
126 of this book. None of Mallarmé's *Poëmes d'Enfance et de Jeunesse* (1858–1863) nor his *Vers de Circonstance* are included here, but the remarkable poem
Un Coup de dés jamais n'abolira le hasard (first published in the magazine *Cosmopolis* in 1897) has been
included, with as faithful a reproduction as our format
permits of the visual layout on which Mallarmé lav-
ished so much thought and care, because its typograph-

ical experiment seems so germane to much of what has followed in subsequent modern poetry. Monsieur Mauron graciously provided for this edition some additional commentaries, and we are grateful as well to his English translators, Messers Julian and Quentin Bell. Readers who wish to go on to a complete, scholarly edition of Mallarmé are referred to the superb *Pléiade* edition, the *Oeuvres Complètes* in one thin-paper volume edited by Henri Mondor and G. Jean-Aubry and now published by Gallimard in Paris.

EDITORIAL NOTE (1936)

THE GENERAL PLAN of this volume is explained in the Introduction. Our authority for the text of the translations has been Roger Fry's corrected typescripts, where these existed, his manuscripts where the poems had not been typed. *Herodias*, *Little Air*, *All The Soul Indrawn*, and *Anguish* are taken from a manuscript book which may be as old as July 1921.

For the most part we have been careful to keep to what appeared to be Roger Fry's final recension of the translation. In a number of poems, however, it has been necessary to choose between alternative versions of the same line or phrase. This was particularly the case in the *Faun*. We have also considered ourselves justified in correcting a few mistranslations of the sense.

The text of the "Early Introduction" by Roger Fry has been reconstituted from three manuscripts, one of them clearly a rough draft. Passages from this incorporated in the text are marked as such. This old introduction was considered inadequate by Roger Fry, and was superseded by that now introducing the book. But the earlier, giving his view of the nature of poetry, is clearly far too important to be omitted. It is printed at the end of this edition.

The short note on *Sigh* is one of an incomplete series of early date, written by Roger Fry, and since superseded by the Commentaries.

The remaining prose is the work of Charles Mauron. The Introduction has been translated by Mrs. K. John; the Commentaries on *Another Fan, The Tomb of Poe, The Swan, All The Soul Indrawn, Little Air, Herodias, The mass of hair a flame's flight, Saint,* and the *Tomb of Verlaine* have been translated by Julian Bell. The remaining Commentaries were translated by Roger Fry.

We have jointly revised the whole book, and done our utmost to present the reader with a correct and comprehensible text and commentary.

CHARLES MAURON
JULIAN BELL

INTRODUCTION

THE FIRST CONVERSATION I ever had with Roger Fry turned, by a happy chance, on Mallarmé. Fourteen years later, at our last meeting, we were arranging the final details of this book. In the meantime, ties beyond price had been formed between us, which seemed to become closer every day, and which death has now severed. I shall not attempt, here, to describe that exalted comradeship. But since it is customary, on the threshold of a book like this, to indicate how it was produced and why, from what materials and with what object, I should like first and foremost to acknowledge the debt of this to intellectual friendship — of all forms of human intercourse indisputably the most humane, since no difference of age, class or nationality can seriously interfere with it.

The initial idea of the book was Roger Fry's entirely. He was so sociable that he could never enjoy anything without at once feeling the need to share it with those around him. Therein lay, I think, the secret of that equilibrium which to the last prevented him from growing old: the correction of fastidiousness by generosity, and of generosity by fastidiousness. Without touching on his private life, which displayed the same balance, one can hardly fail to see how this alternation governed his double life as artist and critic. Struck by some beauty, he turned at once to others, to his friends, to the public, eager to communicate, ready to help, admittedly rather discouraged at moments, but hopeful all the same, deliberately, magnificently credulous ('after all, why should they not learn to be happy?'), and sometimes rewarded. For the number of people indebted to him for an increased sensibility to the pleasures of life is incredible when you consider the difficulty of the undertaking.

To return, then, to my subject — one of his greatest pleasures was in poetry, and especially the poetry of Mallarmé. He made no secret of the difficulties he met with: who does not meet them? But he of all men — he, who was ever on the trail of some new splendour — felt himself attracted by the mysterious 'miroitement en dessous,' which, imprisoned in the poet's most cryptic verses, at once exasperates and delights the mind. And what could not fail to cement his attachment to Mallarmé (he scarcely ever travelled without a copy in his luggage) was the unmistakable sincerity of the artist. Unlike some of his imitators, Mallarmé repels but never disappoints: if the 'miroitement en dessous' does not always give up its secret, at least it is never gratuitous, a mere stage trick.

Assured, then, of an authentic pleasure, Roger Fry's first impulse was to share it: he was charmed, he set himself to translate. His reactions were immediate. But they were so numerous that the comings and goings in his nervous system might be compared to the traffic of a

2

great city, in which thousands of miracles, renewed every second, cannot always prevent certain delays which excite universal indignation. The translation, dropped and resumed according to circumstances, lasted at least twenty years, perhaps more. However, when in 1920 I had the privilege of seeing it for the first time, two-thirds of the poems here presented had acquired more or less their final shape. Every three months or so, a word would be scratched out, another inscribed, thoughtfully, in the little book I was to see so often — until that day when, oh horror! it was filched at the Gare St. Lazare by an unlucky thief. I would have given a good deal for a glimpse of the thief's soul, clouded by the revelation of those 'sibylline sobs,' so hard to turn into cash at any ordinary dealer's. Did he renew the sarcasm and abuse once showered on this poet so freely? Or was there thenceforth in the world another *Mallarmist?* We shall never know. For the little book never returned to the hands of its owner.

But Roger Fry, in his distress, discovered with Proust that lost time can be found again. Hardly had he begun, with a piety like that of Isis, to reassemble in his memory the now scattered members of his work, when the friendly members gathered of their own accord. I was there and can bear witness. The 'sein brûlé d'une antique Amazone' returned from Holland: the swan flew from Sicily and the Venetian lustre from the 6th arrondissement: the Faun hurried down the slopes of our Alpilles:

3

as for the 'sourire du pâle Vasco,' it started up from who knows where. Within a week the text was there, complete, improved even, before Roger Fry's delighted eyes. 'I am robbed and I gain by it,' he said. 'Decidedly, Mallarmé pays.'

Why, then, was he so slow in publishing a work which might be said to be finished? In the first place, from artistic scruples; he might be loaded with work, but would not botch it. But he was withheld also by another consideration: he had always believed in the necessity of adding to the English version of Mallarmé, most difficult of writers, an explanatory text — introduction and commentary; and this task he never had leisure to undertake in earnest. Among his unfinished writings have been found, besides an ironic epigraph,[1] the beginning of a preface, and some explanatory notes, probably very old. In 1930, anxious to have done with it, and with more and more work of all kinds on his hands, he asked me to act as commentator instead of him. In this collaboration, a few words and a smile

---

[1] "Shakespeare in Elysium — question about the meaning of a passage: 'I marvel nothing so much as that men will gird themselves at discovering obscure beauties in an author. Certes the greatest and most pregnant beauties are ever the plainest and most evidently striking; and when two meanings of a passage can in the least ballance [sic] our judgements which to prefer, I hold it matter of unquestionable certainty that neither of them is worth a farthing.' " — HENRY FIELDING in A Journey from this World to the Next.

settled the much talked-of division of labour. 'I will finish the translation,' he said, 'but after all, my dear Charles, the explanation of French poetry is your business.' To this attitude he ever afterwards adhered. It is true that we always worked together, freely comparing our impressions. But the reader must understand the situation: for all that he cannot fail to admire in the translation of the poems Roger Fry is responsible,[2] while I alone am to blame for any imperfections and errors in the commentary.

I do not mean to attempt here anything like a complete study of Mallarmé's poetry. I am undertaking something much more limited. This book, as I have said, had in Roger Fry's mind no object but to give others a share in his own pleasure; but whether the reader approaches Mallarmé's poems in the original or in the English translation, he will come up against the same obstacle — the poet's obscurity. Indeed, it is as though, in spite of the translator's efforts, or rather in proportion to his fidelity, Mallarmé, in half his works at least, still persisted in speaking a foreign language. Foreign in French to a Frenchman, he remains foreign to an Englishman in English. Or rather, it is the reader who feels as though he had suddenly become a foreigner.

[2] Certain turns of phrase which I should call happy if I were not incompetent to judge are, however, due to the suggestions of Julian Bell. As Roger Fry confided to me his express intention of making this acknowledgment, I take the liberty of doing so in his stead.

All who remember the day when first they looked into the *Poems* or the *Divagations* will testify to that curious feeling of *exclusion* which put them, in face of a text written with *their* words (and moreover, as they could somehow feel, magnificently written), suddenly outside their own language, deprived of their rights in a common speech, and, as it were, rejected by their oldest friends. Larousse's *Twentieth Century Dictionary* (in six volumes), published not long ago, bluntly declares that, with the exception of a few fine lines, the poems of Mallarmé are unintelligible. With the reader's permission, we shall decline to accept the opinion of a dictionary, even of a twentieth-century dictionary in six volumes, as the last word in criticism; yet we should be wrong simply to dismiss it with contempt, or to refuse to recognise its significance. For the statement does, in fact, reflect a common view, formed in the poet's lifetime, discredited, I admit, by journalistic expressions of it, but nevertheless founded on the experience of men who knew how to read, and whom it would be rather hasty to call stupid. I may add that if it is a view still held today, thirty-five years after the death of Mallarmé, this is no doubt due in part to intellectual inertia, but also to the fact that experiments yield the same results. The young students of today do not find Mallarmé much easier than their elders did. But their opinion of him has been modified, and above all they make distinctions: they admit, in general, the poet's greatness: they know that his earlier works, from the *Guignon* to the *Hérodiade*, are at once accessible and beautiful: but most of the *Sonnets*, and even the *Après-Midi d'un Faune*, the *Prose pour des Esseintes*, the *Coup de Dés* and the greater part of the *Divagations*, are still more or less foreign to them. A few have succeeded in scaling the defences and reaching a more intimate knowledge of the poet: they know that it was not without effort, that it took a long time and much amused persistence. And even then they can never be sure of their results. Most, however, anxious to admire Mallarmé at any price, either from an instinctive feeling or from esthetic snobbery, cling to the idea that clearness is not essential to poetry, that beauty may be apparent (some say 'is apparent chiefly') in the obscurest works. But the obscurity remains a fact.

This last remark brings us to a question which it will be well to clear up without delay, at least provisionally: is the obscurity which prevails in certain of Mallarmé's works *intentional*? If it is, any pretension to throw light on them becomes not merely idle but impertinent. We may reply to this question with some confidence, because Mallarmé himself dealt with it on more than one occasion, of course in a general form. Part at least of the obscurity which so confounds us was intentional, in fact most deliberately planned. Mystery was, in Mallarmé's view, one of the poet's instruments; the writer, no less than the painter or musician, asserts his title to make use of it, and to distribute it through his work as he thinks fit, for a given purpose. No one asks Rembrandt to define sharply and clearly, 'in an imperturbable foreground,' those contours which of set purpose he has drowned in shadow; no one requires Beethoven or Wagner to develop their theme immediately, at the very moment when they are sedulously burying it in an abyss of music. Half-lights are a part of art, and all psychological expressions of them — presentiments, allusions, echoes, suggestions, memories more or less confused, vibrations more or less remote from the fundamental note have their place in the twilight world of poetry, where information is at most accessory. Perfect clearness befits a statement of fact, a rule of conduct, or a chain of reasoning. But suppose the artist wishes to communicate what we may call, for the sake of brevity, a state of mind. Certain parts of that state of mind remain obscure, and that obscurity seems not only natural, and to be respected for precision's sake (an echo or a hint robbed of its vagueness ceases from that moment to be hint or echo), but, moreover, esthetically necessary. In literature, as in music or in painting, the third dimension is composed of allusions, increasingly uncertain. What the artist does not expressly state, but hints, insinuates, suggests — that is what creates alike depth and distance.

Here, then, we have the obscurity which Mallarmé intended his work to possess, and which should be left

8

intact, at least by those who aspire only to an esthetic pleasure. But there still remains obscurity which was not intended, and which, as I shall try to show, proceeds simply from the conditions in which the poet lived and thought. If he seems to be writing a foreign tongue, it is because he was really and truly a foreigner. He lived, and above all thought, in a foreign mode. His experiences, which he puts into words with the scrupulous care of a man for whom writing is the essential act of life, simply do not, as a rule, correspond to our experiences. For him, I am convinced, they were natural to obviousness. One of the obscurest of his works at a first reading is the lecture on 'Music and Letters' which he gave successively at Oxford and Cambridge. How can we suppose that a man by no means given to hoaxing, professing the sincerest admiration for the universities whose guest he was, lecturing, moreover, on the subject he had most at heart, should have failed to make every effort to be understood, that is, appreciated? Alas! to a reader familiar with the text, the lecturer's ingenuousness becomes almost painfully obvious: for the amusement of the audience, his choicest pleasantries, his most graceful digressions, are intermingled with his beloved meditations upon art: but pleasantries and meditations, being pure Mallarmé, having just the strange turn of his mind, must have appeared, even to that élite of English publics, equally incomprehensible.

9

Who was to blame? No one. All who knew Mallarmé bear witness to his exquisite courtesy; and he himself said that the first duty of a writer was, 'in deference to those whose language, after all, he borrows,' to compose works that should mean something, 'though that be all.' But another duty, at least as imperative, bound him to transcribe his thought with the greatest possible fidelity. Now these obligations may sometimes be mutually exclusive. Every exchange presupposes a mean term, experiences in common. Mallarmé, in addressing his public, even while he reserved the right to make his own use of literary chiaroscuro, always believed himself to be on this common ground with them. He was often genuinely mistaken. Between the meditative existence he pursued behind the curtain of smoke which rose incessantly from his pipe, and the existence of others, a gulf unsuspected by himself had been slowly widening. We find it easier to accept this mutual incomprehension between human beings whose outward experience has been very different: for instance, between a surgeon and a mystic philosopher, or, more simply, between a man and a woman. At least, we protest, if these persons can find a common subject of conversation, they will speak in approximately the same way. But we forget that in Mallarmé's life the great experience was precisely a way of speaking, the exact reflection of a way of thinking personal to himself. So that, 'annonçât-il se moucher,' as he says himself, he announces it unlike other people; the common experience seems to be that of blowing or not blowing one's nose, his is a personal way of seeing such a man blowing his nose.

Confronted with a man who, willy-nilly, can never speak 'like everybody else,' readers may react very differently: some will laugh or be angry, some will be indifferent, some, again, intrigued. I write, of course, only for these last. What can they do? The first impulse, the easiest approach, is to look on Mallarmé's poems as a series of riddles. This would not be a novelty in literature. The poets of the sixteenth century had a passion for riddles. In the eighteenth, the classic example is the Abbé Delille. When he writes:

> 'Le puissant agaric qui du sang épanché
> Arrête les ruisseaux, et dont le sein fidèle
> Du caillou pétillant arrête l'étincelle,' [3]

he is simply asking us a riddle. What is 'le puissant agaric'? Answer: tinder. It is possible to treat certain lines of Mallarmé's in the same way. What is 'Of scintillations at once the septet'? Answer: the Great Bear. Or again, what is the 'Blazon of mourning scattered on vain walls'? Answer: the silver tears on funeral

[3] 'The powerful agaric that stops the streams
Of flowing blood, and in its faithful breast
Adopts the flame leapt from the sparkling stone.'

[In eighteenth-century France the dried stem of a species of agaric was used for tinder, and also to staunch wounds.]

11

cloths. Which cannot fail to suggest the following comments: first, this little trick is unworthy of a true poet; and secondly, its results are singularly limited. And in fact, riddles of this kind are much rarer in Mallarmé than has been supposed; moreover, their solution, as a rule, illuminates only the zone of obscurity *meant* by the poet. Let me emphasise this point. Mallarmé never wished like Delille to pique his readers' curiosity; if he sometimes made use of a subtle definition, not so much *instead of* as *beside* the precise term, it was because he thought it more poetical, not more ingenious. If he had wished to mention the Great Bear he would, I believe, have called it simply the Great Bear. His expression translates something quite different: the sparkling of its beams, and the sort of musical chord which they form. The fact that this chord has a well-known name, useful to astronomers and navigators, is, poetically, quite irrelevant; that is why the name is not given. I could quote twenty examples of the kind. Consider the end of this well-known sonnet:

> 'Dis si je ne suis pas joyeux
> Tonnerre et rubis aux moyeux
> De voir dans l'air que ce feu troue
>
> Avec des royaumes épars
> Comme mourir pourpre la roue
> Du seul vespéral de mes chars.' [4]

---

[4] *'To Get Myself Into Your Story'* (page 120). [see opposite]

What is this wheel? Three interpretations seem to me equally valid: the disc of the setting sun, the wheel of a cab, and the wheel of a firework. Which is right? Perhaps none; perhaps two, merged in a single image. Here also, poetically, the uncertainty matters little. The impression being that of a gorgeous triumphal car (ironical, however, in my opinion), all the words, precisely, combine to establish it; while the material object on which it was built, being without interest of its own, remains in shadow. Suppose I agree that the triumphal chariot was a cab: yet, from the purely poetical standpoint, as soon as the vainglorious hero of the sonnet enters it, the cab is a cab no longer; quite logically the vehicle disappears and gives place to the triumph.

If all Mallarmé's difficulties were of this order, neither Roger Fry nor myself would ever have thought of adding to the poems formal glosses. Precise or vague, obscure or clear, a work of art is what it is; one may like it or not, to modify it would be ridiculous. But, as I have said, Mallarmé's unintentional obscurity is at once more profound and, in a sense, more regrettable. It derives from the strangeness of a mode of thought turned back

---

'Say if I am not joyous
Thunder and rubies at the axles
To see in this fire-pierced air

Amid scattered realms
As though dying purple the wheel
Of my sole chariot of evening.'

upon itself. This strangeness, when diminished by familiarity, becomes, as it were, a charm the more, a sort of intellectual exoticism; but so long as it persists in unmodified sharpness, it shuts us out from the beauty of the poems.

The real question for the reader, then, is less to solve riddles than to get used to a way of thinking which is very unlikely to be his own. Some of those who open this book will already be well acquainted with Mallarmé, and will have performed this labour on their own account. But others, perhaps, will be attempting it for the first time. For me, therefore, the question is whether I can help them. Not open new horizons, nor dispense professorial riches — but, as simply as possible, help them, effacing myself afterwards before the poems, which alone matter.

The essence of what I can say to this effect has its place in the notes, which are concrete, precise, detailed even to pedantry — a pedantry for which I am quite willing to be laughed at if there is the least chance of its being useful. But a few general considerations ought, I think, to precede them. Here they are in brief.

A man may be said to be characterised by his obsessions. Our attention, far from extending uniformly over the whole of our experience, is always concentrated on a few chosen points. These points interest us: we neglect the others. What determines this choice? The psychologists may reply; I wish only to indicate the fact. Our obsessions no doubt enable us to see more clearly whatever their light is focussed on, but they also dazzle us, and blind us to what lies in shadow on either side. When men fail to understand each other, it is often simply for this reason: their obsessions do not coincide. If we examine Mallarmé's early poems, of which Roger Fry has translated only a few, we cannot fail to be struck by the extreme narrowness of his literary field of vision. With two or three exceptions, these poems have in fact only one subject: the author's painful sterility. He wants to write; he knows he can write, for his earliest poems are masterly; but he does not know what about. The obsession which preoccupies him at this time, and by which he is truly 'possessed,' in the magical sense of the term, is neither more nor less than the sheet of white paper ('The empty paper which its whiteness protects') [5] lying in the circle of lamplight. We have no doubt, needless to say, that the 'defender' of that fascinating virginity is the poet himself. He wants to write, but only *what signifies*. Now what signifies does not yet exist. Later it will be a certain form of reverie, essentially Mallarméan, which he alone was capable of producing, but which, at that time, was yet unborn, and which he was protecting before its birth. The narrowness of his field of vision is due, then, to his refusals, and his refusals to an instinctive caution. He

[5] See page 55.

15

rejects alike the sources of interest offered to the writer by outer and inner, by the world and the soul. The life which surged round him at this period is the same that rolls tumultuously through the novels of Zola — the second Empire, the war, the Commune: at thirty he was fairly well acquainted with Paris, London, and the life of the French provinces: and of all this he retains nothing for his work. (We may ask, in passing, whether Mallarmé did not 'live' solely out of politeness — teaching English, out of politeness to society which provided him with food and shelter; giving, out of politeness, to those who asked, apparently, poems, fashion articles, an advertisement for gas, a memorial notice, a newspaper serial, or a box of chocolates with a rose-pink ribbon and a rose-pink verse — all his activity, outside his mental life, seems to have reduced itself to what he himself calls a 'salut, exact, de part et d'autre.') His defences are no less firm on the literary side; he is hardly touched even by the influence of Baudelaire. Finally, he allows himself no great lyrical outbursts. The fact is, what he feels and what he sees are alike, for him, part of reality. And he does not want reality for his white page. He wants, and above all he will want, *something else.* I entreat the reader to remember that 'something else,' for it will become the heart of our interpretation.

But as yet the *something else* is unborn, and the white page remains white, or nearly so. For Mallarmé, obsessed finally as much by his fight against impotence as by the 'virgin paper,' cannot abstain from noting on it certain moments of what he calls his 'agony.' These first poems give us some idea of the cruelty of the struggle. 'Cruel art,' 'the cruel ideal,' are habitual expressions; the dominant notion is that of escape: escape through brute insensibility:

'I ask of your bed heavy sleep without dreams.'
(*Anguish*)

escape through adventure:

'But oh my heart listen to the sailor's song'
(*Sea Breeze*)

escape through opium reveries, vaguely sad and musical, children's dreams and lost paradises, full of flowers, of viols and of sobs:

'Seraphim in tears
Dreaming, bow in hand, in the calm of vaporous
Flowers,'
(*Apparition*)

escape through the dream of an art made easy by tradition:

'I would leave the voracious art of a cruel
Country . . .
Imitate the Chinese of clear delicate heart'
(*Tired of the Bitter Repose*)

escape, finally, through death, always at hand, in flower-chalices, in lust, and in the extreme lassitude of autumn.

1 7

Cemeteries, graves, poisons, hangings, shipwrecks, nothingness — the enumeration (absurd here) of words barely insinuated in the poems themselves, none the less testifies to the persistence of an idea which would certainly have given a psychoanalyst (had psycho-analysts existed in those days) great concern. The analyst would also, I think, have noted certain outbursts of an eroticism curiously negatived elsewhere,[6] and the poet's ambiguous attitude to a life of instinct,[7] which at times he seems to regret, assimilating it to the Eden-purity of morning:

> 'A glory for which I once fled the adorable
> Childhood of roses and woods'

and which at other times he curses for its omnipresent irony.

These struggles, which no one that I am aware of has ever brought to the notice of the experts, seem to me the reflection (or the cause) of the artistic struggle which was going on at the same time in the poet's soul. Roger Fry, in his early preface,[8] emphasises the purity of Mallarmé. Now, at the time of the early poems, the author seems to be still in search of a definition of pure art —

[6] Unfortunately there is little trace of it in the earliest poems translated. Cf. in the French section: *Une négresse, Tristesse d'été*, etc., and the translation of *Angoisse*.

[7] Roger Fry has pointed out in a note that azure, in Mallarmé's poetry, symbolised this life.

[8] See page 289.

not of an abstract, but of a *living* definition. For he is *living* the drama of the artist who is at the same time a real being, and who has to establish between outer and inner a compromise, a *modus vivendi* of some sort — a state of war or of peace (utilisation, co-operation, or repressions and underhand revenges), interweavings of complex actions and reactions whose result is to be the life and work of the individual, with its victories and disasters. For the fact is that art, pure or impure, has no abstract definition. There is no art. There are only men who are artists, who, at each moment of their lives, are their own definition. The opposition between pure and impure thus resolves itself into a difference of accent and, if I may repeat it, of obsessions; the more the interest is concentrated on the work and not on its materials, which obviously come from outside it, the purer the artist. The novelist who merely copies the world, the lyric poet who merely copies his soul, is impure, because the aspect of the world or of his soul preoccupies him more than the aspect of his book. Conversely, when Flaubert or Mallarmé, transposing the terms, feels that after all the world or his soul exists only to be translated into words, he has reached the other limit of the definition.

The odd thing is that esthetic meditation, in its search for purity, almost always begins by harping on what wounds it, what must be excluded: reality, it declares, must not invade the page or the canvas, sacred as these are to 'something else.' So we have reality turned out. But at first the page and the canvas remain empty. Ask an artist who has just found out that the 'subject' of a work doesn't matter: 'Very well! what does?' He will not quite know. What obsesses him is nothing positive. He wants 'something else,' or nothing. For the moment he cherishes that nothing, which he has won by main force and which he feels continually threatened. For reality is imperialist; Nature abhors a vacuum. To preserve the vacuum, the clean sheet — such was, undoubtedly, Mallarmé's essential preoccupation at the time of his writing the *Hérodiade*.

It is the most accessible, and consequently the best known of Mallarmé's great poems. The *Hérodiade* seems to have been whole years in hand; the second part, the *Cantique de St. Jean*, strikes one as very much later than the beginning; and the *Finale* announced by the poet was never written at all, that I know of. The technique even of the first part is by no means uniform; certain lines, like:

> 'Know you not a land
> Where the sinister sky has the hated looks
> Of Venus who, the eve long, burns in the leafage';

recall, though with an accent more convulsed, more hostile to natural life, those of the *Faune*:

'A festival glows in the leafage extinguished:
  Etna! 'tis amid you, visited by Venus
  On your lava fields placing her candid feet, . . .'

Others, as:

              'Light, too, it's childish
  You'll say, those torches where wax with subtle fire
  Weeps mid the vain gold some strange tear'

have a kind of relaxed softness very unlike the hard
gem-like brilliances amassed elsewhere. In short, the
Hérodiade everywhere betrays rehandling, indecision,
an absence of unity confirmed by its interruption, and
explained clearly, in my opinion, by the amazing psychological transformation which the poet underwent in the
space of a few years.

The beginning of the *Hérodiade* translated here (for
we know of an older version), probably dates from
about the time of his Tournon appointment. It closes
what I may call the 'period of conflict' in Mallarmé's
art. His obsession with an of course purely literary
virginity has now become so intense that it takes shape
as a phantom: and what a cloudy phantom! The least
movement, the mere idea of a voluptuous perfume, the
mere evocation of a 'mortal' sends Herodias into con-
vulsions of alarm. Here, too, the psychoanalyst would
have something to say; this savage modesty is too un-
easy. Twice, moreover, we glimpse in the depths of her

soul that repressed desire which — far more than the innocent Nurse — is her real and powerful enemy. Look at the invocation to the mirror:

> 'But ah! Some evenings in your severe fount
> I of my sparse dreams have known the nudity.'

and at the end of the poem the avowal:

> 'You lie, naked flower
> Of my lips. I await a thing unknown.'

Herodias, at first a symbol of absolute purity, thus becomes in spite of herself the symbol of a purity yielding and disintegrating. Yielding to what? To the *Après-Midi d'un Faune*.

Nothing could be more striking than the change of atmosphere from one poem to the other, especially when we consider that they were conceived at almost the same time.[9] That of Herodias is deliberately sparkling and icy:

> 'White night of ice-clots and cruel snow,'

or at least tends to be so. That of the Faun, mellow as a Venetian canvas, at once calm and sensual, is permeated with warm airs and erotic suggestions. No more whiteness (apparently at least), no hint of cruelty, of virginity still less, save in the guise of a titillating innocence. It is impossible to doubt that the Mallarmé of the *Après-Midi* is a happy poet, the poet of a suc-

[9] The *Après-Midi* was first published in 1876.

cessful inner life. What has happened? 'Something else' — at once a dream and the technique of its expression, what the psychoanalysts call 'sublimation,' a way of poetic life, a way of using reality instead of repulsing it. The world has become, in Mallarmé's own expression, 'transfusible en du songe.' The key to this literary alchemy is to liquefy, evaporate reality into a sort of potential gold — a happy dream — which, it may be, does not exist, but which for that very reason is 'something else' than all that does. A passage on music in *Divagations* gives us an exact description of the process:

> 'Observe, the instruments detach, with a spell easy to surprise, the summit of natural landscapes, vaporise and anew combine them, floating, in a higher state. See how, to express the forest, merged in twilight green horizon, there needs only such a chord, where the chase barely is remembered: or the meadow, the waning afternoon's pastoral fluidity, is now glassed and gone in river-echoes. A line, a few brief vibrations, the suggestion is complete.'

That this miracle, familiar to all symphony-lovers, can be realised with words as well as notes, we shall presently see; for the technique of the spell — every artistic miracle has its technique — is closely connected with that obscurity of style which is my main subject here. First let us observe its importance and its meaning; let the 'sublimation' be applied, not in this case to 'natural landscapes,' but to the landscape of Mallarmé's soul, to the obsessions which the early poems have revealed to us — and immediately we have the essence of the *Après-Midi*. An erotic obsession, a literary obsession: such are the two summits of that landscape. And both are here 'transfused' into dream. The amorous desires of the Faun do not attain physical satisfaction, in the first place because he is only dreaming, and secondly because when the evocation becomes too sharp the nymphs again become phantoms, slip from his arms and disappear. And then it is in the notes of the syrinx, in the weaving of metaphorical and musical 'confusions,' that the demi-god finds consolation; the syrinx, 'instrument of flights.' The other modes of escape, all in some way painful, are no longer even thought of, since the only one really desired, the mode of art, has at length succeeded. The Faun effects on his own desires a liberating transposition; he 'evaporates' the naked female forms which obsess him into a musical arabesque. I want to make, he says:

> 'Die out of the everyday dream of a back
> Or a pure flank followed by my curtained eyes,
> An empty, sonorous, monotonous line.'

What were, for the poet himself, the conditions of this reconciliation? Doubtless, above all, greater happiness. Greater abandonment, perhaps, to an eroticism essential to his nature; an increase of epicurism, favoured by the atmosphere of a city rich in pleasures of all kinds — galleries, books, theatres, human intercourse; an increase, too, of self-confidence — Mallarmé while still a young man was recognised, at least by his peers, as one of the great writers of his generation, and the assurances of this which reached him in Paris, the admiration and interest excited by his earliest works, could hardly fail to soften and please him, at least to drive away the nightmare of sterility which had pursued him hitherto. And finally, I shall add to these hypothetical but, I think, very probable influences one more, important precisely for its frivolity — the fashion articles which the poet was writing in 1874 and 1875, just before the appearance of the *Faune*. That Mallarmé, imaginatively clothing the bodies of girls and young women (some of whom were his correspondents) in *tulle illusion* and floral ornaments, experienced a subtle erotic pleasure, seems to me unquestionable. It would have been abnormal if he had not; from the very dawn of civilisation, feminine dress has been part of the love-display. But he was attracted as a poet also; he learned here, in the first place, a set of metaphors afterwards confirmed by his regular attendance at the ballet. Secondly, and above all, he gained a power of observing the outer world carefully but not quite seriously, a lighter, gayer touch, a taste for the essential trifles, an abandonment to the wildest flights of fancy, as in the following sketch, grotesque yet acute, of Anglo-Saxon tourists in the days of Victoria: 'Nomads, both men and women, their white veils lifted, to be rolled, like a light portable tent, around their hats; their lorgnettes, re-calling the astronomer-herdsman of Chaldea, each returned carefully to its leather sheath.'

Mallarmé is happy; Mallarmé is enjoying himself. He will always enjoy himself henceforth; only his diver-sions will become more unlike ours. At present let us observe that his paradise is no longer behind him, in the morning purity of a life of instinct which he re-jected long ago for the life of art, but before or rather above him, in those higher regions where, for his amuse-ment alone, reigns 'something else.' In the course of his Oxford and Cambridge lecture, Mallarmé calls the poet 'ce civilisé édenique'; the same Eden reappears in the *Toast Funèbre à Théophile Gautier*, not as a lost paradise — that conflict has been resolved — but as an ideal garden where the poet is securely established in his double function of angel Gabriel and pacific park-keeper.

Now let us return to the literary technique of these first sublimations. Arising out of an equal disgust with romanticism and naturalism, this 'transposition,' as Mallarmé calls it, 'from the fact to the idea,' this evapo-ration of reality into a sort of musically fluid dream, preoccupied the whole symbolist generation. Verlaine and Rimbaud are both haunted by it in their wander-ings, at the time of the *Romances sans Paroles*. The

26

method follows clearly from the aim in view. The poem must be lightened as much as possible; the ideal, therefore, is to give, like the 'Chinese of clear delicate heart,' only the essentials — a few strokes here and there, the sky, the lake, the moon, three reeds; and the sky is a bare china-blue. 'A line, a few brief vibrations, the suggestion is complete.' Naturally, to make up, each stroke must be of incredible precision: hence an impressionism pushed to the extreme. So we have already two causes of obscurity; it is easy to become obscure if one says too little of too personal an experience. Neither Rimbaud nor even Verlaine is always free from this reproach; how much we should miss in their poetry if we had not learnt from other sources the events of their life! But that is not all. The same object of lightening the style requires the use of words which, far from grasping reality like those of Flaubert, for example, just brush against it, and allude rather than state. Verlaine gives a literary recipe, indeed, to this effect:

> 'Also you must never go
> To choose words without some mistake.'

Plain terms are eliminated: the writer is deliberately aiming just beside the mark: each word brushes lightly by what it would suggest, and the sentence advances, dissolves, unfettered by anything precise or heavy. The 'mistake' of which Verlaine speaks is simply, after all, a metaphor sketched in a single word. If the term em-

2 7

ployed does not frankly represent one of our experiences, the reason is that it aims at representing two, or several; it skims this, but glides obliquely towards that, like those discords in music which, harmonising with what went before, are already looking to what is to follow. We thus gain in movement what we lose in exactness. The height of success for these 'deliberately false' words is to appear on reflection juster than any others, nearer a real experience whose fluidity would be lost in common speech. Thus we have in Verlaine:

> 'L'allée est sans fin
> Sous le ciel divin
> D'être pâle ainsi.
> Sais-tu qu'on serait
> Bien sous le secret
> De ces arbres-ci?' [10]

Three strokes of the brush: the avenue, the sky, the invitation: two evasive terms — *sans fin, secret*: a persistent suggestion of the real — *ainsi, ces arbres-ci*. And how *right* is the whole thing!

The *Après-Midi d'un Faune* offers numberless examples of this technique. Yet Mallarmé is not really like

[10] 'The avenue is endless
Under the sky enchanted
By being so pale.
You know, we should be
Happier, hidden
Under those trees.'

either Verlaine or Rimbaud; he is, it must be owned, much more obscure. Why is that? The impressionist technique I have outlined leads naturally to an art rather thin and discontinuous. But in Mallarmé two tendencies, at least, opposed this kind of slenderness. First, the strength of his eroticism, which naturally becomes a love of solid form: the poet certainly wishes to avoid sharp contours, but, like Renoir, will have rich and full colour none the less. Compare Verlaine's *Allée*, with its harmonious but simple colouring, to the underwoods of the *Faune*, where the nymphs' flesh-colour plays in an 'air heavy with tufted slumbers': it is the difference between a water-colour and an oil-painting. To this love of solidity we must add a love of long arabesques, rising, falling, rising again, like the flute solo which actually opens Debussy's transcription of the *Faune*. In short, the art of the 'Chinese of clear delicate heart' does not suit Mallarmé. He had in him something of the great 'baroque' artists: a passion for vast wave-like diagonals, for sentences running from end to end of the work, as is shown by the structure of many poems, even without counting the endless unfolding of the *Coup de Dés*. If, then, he merely skims reality, it will be in passing with gentle continuity from one object to the next. His brush, if I may so express it, leaves the canvas as seldom as possible; he does not put in a touch here and a touch there, but traces long sequences of which each is a whole. At the end of the sentence, a white space; then a new sentence, no less rich than its predecessor. Grammatically, this involves a degree of complication well calculated to increase obscurity. Verlaine's sentence is always simple: Mallarmé's is full of subtle convolutions; and as the poetic arabesque, precisely determined by gliding passages from one reality to another, is quite distinct from the syntactical order, the latter, suppled, bent, dislocated for purposes other than its own, is not restored without considerable difficulty.[11] Such, then, at the time of the *Après-Midi d'un Faune*, were the causes of an obscurity unavoidable, in my opinion (for what Mallarmé had to say could not have been said otherwise), but yet an obstacle to the reader: a lightening of the style, hence a noting only of essentials; an attempt to catch exactly the spontaneous impression; a use of what at first seem the wrong words, so as to allow of metaphorical obliquities, and subtlety and fluidity of thought; finally, the drawing of long arabesques. The scholiast's task (and every reader is, as such, a scholiast) seems therefore plain. He must, if he can, supply what is not stated (for example, that the Faun awakes and has been dreaming of nymphs); restate in familiar terms too personal impressions (explain, for instance, that the 'light carnation' is an impression of the dream nymphs superimposed, on waking, on a background of the underwood);

[11] The same idea is expressed by Roger Fry in his early introduction. See pages 300–301.

correct or rather analyse what seem to be wrong terms ('tufted slumbers' = sleepy and tufted forest), and finally, restore the syntactical order. That is, of course, when some obscurity requires it. A complicated piece of work, the reader will say. I agree with him. But I should like to point out that Mallarmé is not the only writer who demands it of us. All poems, more or less, if they are to be both understood and appreciated, call for some effort of the kind. A certain gusto may make it an unconscious effort; but if we try to read poetry when our minds are jaded, or in a language not our own (even though we may think ourselves pretty much at home in it), immediately the same difficulties reappear: we stumble at whatever is uncustomary in the poetry (there is always something); the syntax no longer guides us, the ambiguous words lead us astray; and soon we begin to wonder what this infernal poet is getting at.

The years following Mallarmé's installation in Paris in 1873 witness the unfolding of his peculiar genius. He has recovered contact, he has even made a treaty, with reality. He has learnt to use its support, and leap, as from a firm though narrow springboard, elsewhere, towards 'something else.' Henceforth all his poems have an extremely concrete starting-point: the furniture of a bedroom, the curtains of a window, a girl diving, a woman combing her hair. Reassured in this direction, at peace with the world and his soul, he feels free to pursue to the very borders of metaphysics his meditations on the art of writing. Thus the most abstract of painters will paint herrings and apples. There is truly, in the field of esthetics, a logical sequence of thought, a natural trend of the human mind, which causes the most different artists to approach the same problems, one by one, in the same order. When Roger Fry had satisfied himself that the 'subject' in art did not matter, he looked for what did matter and reached in the end his 'systems of relations,' the most abstract of esthetic theories, whose typical work of art is a still life. Mallarmé's thought followed a parallel evolution.

He was naturally pagan. As long as the flesh in him was still at odds with poetry, he called it 'sad': the conflict being now at an end, he finds it cheerful enough, but not of very great importance, and certainly not sinful. On the other hand, he has begun to realise that literary 'sublimations' carry him into 'higher regions,' into a world which seems to him fundamentally more 'real' than the other, because he is more obsessed with it. It was inevitable that the meeting-point of these tendencies should be a kind of platonism. Doubtless Mallarmé's conversations with Villiers de l'Isle-Adam, an ardent Hegelian, did much to aid in the formation of this doctrine. The Faun becomes a philosopher: the Idea makes its appearance.

Here begins a curious chapter in Mallarmé's development, essential from our point of view, which might be entitled: 'Conversation and cross-purposes between a metaphysician and a poet.' I will sketch it only so far as I think necessary for the literal comprehension of the poems.

Mallarmé, in his search for the bases of the literary art, gives to human speech two attributes. The first is what he calls *reportage*. E. M. Forster, in his essay on 'Anonymity,' a marvellously lucid little work, calls this use of language 'information.' The analogy is perfect, and, because undesigned, extremely valuable. But when we come to the second use of language, the divergences begin. E. M. Forster calls it 'creation' — the creation of an atmosphere or a poetic reality — which he admits is almost impossible to define. Mallarmé, on the other hand, says that this second use of language is to pass from the world of the concrete to the world of pure ideas. This passage takes place in two distinct times. First of all, there is the birth of a single pure idea, say that of the 'flower.' 'Je dis: une fleur, et hors de l'oubli où ma voix relègue aucun contour, en tant que quelque chose d'autre que les calices sus, musicalement se lève, idée même et suave, l'absente de tous bouquets.'[12]

Next, by combining such pure ideas, we attain, in theory, to Music (with a capital M), to 'all the relations existing in all,' to the 'intellectual word at its apogee' — in short, to the harmony of platonic Ideas.

[12] That is to say: the mere word *flower* creates an ideal flower obviously absent from all real bouquets, different (here we have the 'something else!') from all known chalices, which rises up precisely because I forget, in its favour, every distinct outline.

E. M. Forster's theory and that of Mallarmé do not at first appear irreconcilable. Indeed Mallarmé would have thought them one and the same: for to him the world of poetic realities was nothing but this platonic world of pure ideas. There, however, in my opinion, lies the fallacy. When I hear of the 'intellectual word at its apogee,' and of 'all the relations existing in all,' what it suggests to me is Einstein's relativity formula, enabling us to pass from one system of co-ordinates to another. Mallarmé says: on the one hand we have 'reporting,' information, on the other 'transposition,' which passes from the fact to the idea. Well, the truths of science are on one hand, indisputably, valuable information, and as such to be ranked under the first use of language; but on the other hand they bear the obvious mark of a mental transposition from concrete to abstract, and therefore should be placed in Mallarmé's second category, side by side with his poems — which would be carrying system rather far. Thus, because it fails to distinguish between science and poetry, Mallarmé's classification breaks down.

The question which then arises is this: if Mallarmé's philosophical theory was unsound, how did he contrive, as a poet, to make such good use of it? By virtue of a fortunate misunderstanding which I shall explain. We were speaking just now of 'pure ideas.' But there is no doubt that for a man of science and for Mallarmé these words mean different things. The former sees in abstraction an advance towards simplicity: for the botanist a 'flower' is the reproductive organ of a certain class of vegetables: and this idea in his mind is much simpler, much better known, than any particular flower he may pick by the roadside. But when Mallarmé says 'a flower,' what is he evoking? The flower 'absent from all bouquets,' the flower we shall never see, shall never pick, a new species of flower, in short, which our senses cannot know, but which rises before our mind from the mere fact of naming it. This new reality is not simpler than the old: it is *different*. It has undergone an extraordinary volatilisation and rarefaction of its sensible qualities; but on the other hand it has grown more complex, for instead of a single object the imagination may vaguely call up a thousand possible objects. In short, abstraction to Mallarmé is only a new means of brushing against reality, of suggesting without stating it. Hence the importance, in the sentence quoted above, of the adverb 'musically' — 'Je dis: une fleur, et, musicalement, se lève l'absente de tous bouquets.' Thus, at a concert, the instruments 'detached the summit of natural landscapes.' Abstraction is a music of thought.

From the point of view of stylistic obscurity, this theory has notable consequences. First, it leads the poet to make use of abstract instead of common nouns: *vol* (flight) instead of *ailes* (wings):

'Ce blanc vol fermé que tu poses.' (*Another Fan*)

35

solitude (solitude) instead of *paysage solitaire* (empty landscape):

> 'Quelconque une solitude.' (*Little Air*)

ıt also leads him to detach qualities from the objects which support them, to endow those qualities with a preponderant, indeed even autonomous existence. In the white paper, the whiteness obsesses him and comes to stand alone; the paper vanishes. The same bent leads him naturally to suppress the real term in a metaphor: of the triumphal cab, that is, the cab resembling a triumphal chariot, we have seen that the second term is left alone. Thus the cloud like a rock becomes 'the black rock' (*Tomb of Verlaine*), and here we reach the limit of the comprehensible.

Another curious result — the most typical, perhaps, of all — of this flight towards poetic abstraction is the obsession with *absence* which gradually invades Mallarmé's poetry. The reader will find it everywhere, from the absence of flowers in the sonnet *A votre chère morte* (astray among the early poems, but really later than the *Après-Midi d'un Faune*) to the absence of breast in the *Antique Amazone*, between which we have the absence of light, the absence of fire, the absence of a bed, and so on, not counting the admirable *Nénuphar Blanc* of the *Divagations*, which I vainly urged Roger Fry to translate. The poet is rowing on a stream with lowered eyes, seeing nothing but the sparkling of water and oars in the sunlight. All at once the boat runs into a clump of reeds. The rower becomes aware that he is in the grounds of a woman he knows. She may even be there, close to him; raising his eyes, he might see her. The silence throbs with every possibility. And to the poet comes the idea of not raising his eyes, of keeping the possibilities intact and going his way with the memory of that moment:

'Advise, my dream, what shall I do?
Sum in a look the virgin absence of this solitude, and as we pluck, in remembrance of a beautiful place, one of those magic lotus-flowers with petals shut, which suddenly rise there, folding in their hollow whiteness a nothing made of inviolate dreams, of the happiness that will not be, and of my breath held now in dread of an appearance, go with it. . . .'

The *Nénuphar Blanc* is clearly almost an exact transcription of the Faun into modern terms (which, be it said in passing, is not without some faint absurdity): the erotic preoccupation is no doubt less open, the mistress of the park being a *clothed* nymph. But how can we fail to recognise her, changeless though arrayed in the height of the fashion of 1875, as in that well-known passage:

'Subtle secrecy of the feet that come and go, convey

the spirit here or there, at the will of the dear shade deep buried in the cambric and lace of a skirt flowing upon the ground.'

Like the Faun, the oarsman (wearing, no doubt, a 'boater,' that 'straw halo') obtains no real satisfaction; like the Faun, he is consoled by the 'hollow whiteness' of a dream. And once more the name of Freud rises to our lips. Observe by what incomparable sleight of artistic genius the whiteness, silence, emptiness, painful obsession of the early poems, at the period when the 'virgin paper' cruelly represented to the poet his own sterility, are transformed to the supreme ideal. The obsession persists, but its sign is changed: from painful it has become pleasant.

The discovery of 'something else' has altered everything, at least in appearance — for we know nothing of the psychological depths of the question. Something other than reality, however, in the last resort is — nothing. And the whole of literature (as Mallarmé, henceforth perfectly lucid, was to explain to the English public in a style at first sight incomprehensible) consists in the play of modulations between these two extremes.

A capital discovery: for if one thinks at all about the conditions of what Roger Fry calls pure art, one cannot fail to see that the first of these conditions is the establishment of a keyboard. There can be no architecture without fixed points and subtle methods of passing from one to another: without the modal system, no Gregorian music: without 'tempered' keyboard, no Bach: without depth and a scale of luminous values, no true painting. And the great creators are those who not merely perform and construct, but in the first place cast their instrument to suit the kind of performance which is proper to them. Mallarmé from the very first knew the two extremes of his own range — crude reality and 'grudging silence'; he suffered because he found himself invariably rejected by each in turn. What he wanted was to write, that is, to make free play from one extremity to the other. A keyboard is nothing but a system of transitions.

We have seen the poet getting at his own system bit by bit. First he detaches himself from reality: the solid grasping, the close embracing of language and experience is transformed into a light musical touch: then the light touch becomes an idea: the idea becomes an absence, and when absence rejoins whiteness, silence, nothingness — the other end of the keyboard has been reached. Henceforth every modulation is possible: the work of art is an arabesque freely traced by the mind between what exists — our experience of the world, outer or inner — and what does not exist, passing through all the gradations of dream.

Every modulation is possible: by that mere idea Mallarmé is intoxicated, for there have been few men more sensitive to what I may call 'the raptures of method.' Immediately, like a mathematician presented with an equation representing an infinite number of possible values, who thereupon examines two or three particularly 'interesting' solutions, the poet sets about finding 'type-modulations': he can evaporate reality into dream, that is an old story; but also, conversely, he may condense dream into reality, start from the vaguest of allusions, and, gradually closing in, alight on some familiar object. All imaginable arabesques may be reduced to combinations of these two.

Such is the dream of the esthetician. Meanwhile the poet is writing the *Éventail de Mlle. Mallarmé*, the *Petits Airs*, and most of the sonnets. Naturally, the obsessions of the theorist will be reflected in them. I always come round to that idea of obsession: the obsession with sterility explains the earlier poems, with musical sublimation, the *Après-Midi d'un Faune*, with a poetic Eden, the *Toast Funèbre:* and the obsession with modulations, in either direction, between daily life and nothing, fills the last poems. Now these successive preoccupations, following one another in a logical curve, or rather in the curve of Mallarmé's experience, become more and more unlike the obsessions we all share; and the increasing obscurity of the poems has no other cause. No doubt it can be reduced in detail to odd turns of speech, remote allusions, ellipses, grammatical peculiarities; but these different kinds of strangeness have a common origin, the thought of which they are the exact expression. They were natural to the author, they become natural to us if we can recapture the author's state of mind.

My task is nearly over, and I shall not say much of the last poems: my notes will deal with them. But one question still detains me: to what extent can we make use of Mallarmé's pronouncements on his art to explain the art itself? When an artist tells us what he meant to do, there is, I think, a great danger — a great temptation to see in his work nothing but his theory. The work is always immeasurably more complex. None of Mallarmé's poems is as simple as the magical formula he appeals to. He may dream of evaporating or condensing reality at pleasure; actually, he is tracing complicated arabesques determined by a variety of conditions: external reality, the associations of familiar ideas, the inspiration of the moment, the exigencies of language, prosody and syntax. With each of these conditions terms may be made, but only certain terms. Like all real poems, the poems of Mallarmé are compromises. Then what precise help do we get from the poet's esthetic theory? Above all, I think, the definition of a spiritual climate. For reasons far more obscure, perhaps, than we suspect, Mallarmé's thought was at ease only in dream, in that intermediate region between reality and the void. There he found employment for all his resources, from his eroticism and his love of common things to a

kind of intellectual sensitiveness, stirred by the slight-
est breath: for his humour, fancy, metaphorical gym-
nastics, and an indescribable airy virtuosity. He was
fond of acrobatic feats, rocket-like sallies, glidings upon
air, and practised them deliberately, asking himself,
whatever spectacle was offered him by the street, the
theatre, or his own home: 'What does this *mean?*'
that is: what arabesque can I trace, through dream,
between the two or three facts which reality here presents to me, and which are to be justified by that
arabesque? For, his obsession being concentrated on the
movement of the mind and not on the actual data, it was
in truth the former which justified the latter: instead of a
curve being the means of relating facts to one another,
the facts were meaningless except as points in an ideal
line. And, of course, nothing could be more fantastic
than these justifying arabesques. The poet, while, as he
said, 'yielding the initiative to the words,' retained
towards them a slightly ironical attitude (irony is a part
of dream, just as are uncertainty and allusiveness), and
we cannot be sure how far he is in jest. It is safest to believe that he is always slightly in jest, sometimes less
than one would suppose, and sometimes more. Whether
he is justifying the veil wrapped round the tourists' hats
by its suggestion of a nomad's tent, or comparing a
woman's hair to the last 'presumptuous' tatter of a vanished sunset, we are in the same free fairy-land atmosphere, now humorous, now poetical. Fairy-land: I beg

the reader to remember that word when he comes to the last poems. One of the greatest obstacles to our understanding of Mallarmé is undoubtedly a refusal to let ourselves go, a sort of stiffening of the mind. If Roger Fry was so intimate and on such good terms with him to the last, perhaps *Alice in Wonderland* had something to do with it.

CHARLES MAURON

POEMS

SALUT

Rien, cette écume, vierge vers
A ne désigner que la coupe;
Telle loin se noie une troupe
De sirènes mainte à l'envers.

Nous naviguons, ô mes divers
Amis, moi déjà sur la poupe
Vous l'avant fastueux qui coupe
Le flot de foudres et d'hivers;

Une ivresse belle m'engage
Sans craindre même son tangage
De porter debout ce salut

Solitude, récif, étoile
A n'importe ce qui valut
Le blanc souci de notre toile.

APPARITION

La lune s'attristait. Des séraphins en pleurs
Rêvant, l'archet aux doigts, dans le calme des fleurs
Vaporeuses, tiraient de mourantes violes
De blancs sanglots glissant sur l'azur des corolles.
— C'était le jour béni de ton premier baiser.

SALUTATION

Nothing! this foam and virgin verse
To designate nought but the cup;
Such, far off, there plunges a troop
Of many Sirens upside down.

We are navigating, my diverse
Friends! I already on the poop
You the splendid prow which cuts
The main of thunders and of winters;

A fine ebriety calls me
Without fear of its rolling
To carry, upright, this toast

Solitude, reef, star
To whatever it was that was worth
Our sail's white solicitude.

APPARITION ✓

The moon was saddening. Seraphim in tears
Dreaming, bow in hand, in the calm of vaporous
Flowers, were drawing from dying violins
White sobs gliding down blue corollas
— It was the blessed day of your first kiss.

Ma songerie aimant à me martyriser
S'enivrait savamment du parfum de tristesse
Que même sans regret et sans déboire laisse
La cueillaison d'un Rêve au cœur qui l'a cueilli.
J'errais donc, l'œil rivé sur le pavé vieilli
Quand avec du soleil aux cheveux, dans la rue
Et dans le soir, tu m'es en riant apparue
Et j'ai cru voir la fée au chapeau de clarté
Qui jadis sur mes beaux sommeils d'enfant gâté
Passait, laissant toujours de ses mains mal fermées
Neiger de blancs bouquets d'étoiles parfumées.

SOUPIR

Mon âme vers ton front où rêve, ô calme sœur,
Un automne jonché de taches de rousseur
Et vers le ciel errant de ton œil angélique
Monte, comme dans un jardin mélancolique,
Fidèle, un blanc jet d'eau soupire vers l'Azur!
— Vers l'Azur attendri d'Octobre pâle et pur
Qui mire aux grands bassins sa langueur infinie
Et laisse, sur l'eau morte où la fauve agonie
Des feuilles erre au vent et creuse un froid sillon,
Se traîner le soleil jaune d'un long rayon.

My dreaming loving to torment me ╰
Was drinking deep of the perfume of sadness
That even without regret and deception is left
By the gathering of a Dream in the heart which has
    gathered it.
I wandered then, my eyes on the worn pavement
When with the sun in your hair, and in the street
In the evening, you in laughter appeared to me
And I thought I saw the fairy with her cap of brightness
Who once on the beauty-sleeps of my spoilt childhood
Passed, letting always her half-closed hands
Snow down white bouquets of perfumed stars.

SIGH

My soul towards your brow where dreams, my calm
    sister,
An autumn scattered with freckles of russet
And the wandering heaven of your angelic eye
Mounts up as in some melancholical gardens
Faithful, a white jet sighs towards the Azure!
— Towards October's tender, pure and pale Azure
Which reflects in great basins its infinite languor
And lets, on dead water where the tawny death-throes
Of leaves wander windswept and scoop a cold furrow,
The yellow sun creep of a long-drawn-out ray.

ANGOISSE

Je ne viens pas ce soir vaincre ton corps, ô bête
En qui vont les péchés d'un peuple, ni creuser
Dans tes cheveux impurs une triste tempête
Sous l'incurable ennui que verse mon baiser:

Je demande en ton lit le lourd sommeil sans songes
Planant sous les rideaux inconnus du remords,
Et que tu peux goûter après tes noirs mensonges,
Toi qui sur le néant en sais plus que les morts:

Car le Vice, rongeant ma native noblesse
M'a comme toi marqué de sa stérilité,
Mais tandis que ton sein de pierre est habité

Par un cœur que la dent d'aucun crime ne blesse,
Je fuis, pâle, défait, hanté par mon linceul,
Ayant peur de mourir lorsque je couche seul.

LAS DE L'AMER REPOS . . .

Las de l'amer repos où ma paresse offense
Une gloire pour qui jadis j'ai fui l'enfance
Adorable des bois de roses sous l'azur
Naturel, et plus las sept fois du pacte dur
De creuser par veillée une fosse nouvelle

ANGUISH

I come not tonight to conquer your body, oh brute
In whom course the sins of a people, nor hollow
In your tresses' impurity a dismal storm
With the fatal ennui that my kisses pour out:

I ask of your bed heavy sleep without dreams
Brooding in curtains unknown of remorse,
Which you too can taste after your black deceits,
You who of Zero know more than the dead:

For Vice, having gnawed by nobleness inborn,
Has marked me like you with its sterility,
But whilst in your breast of stone there is dwelling

A heart that the tooth of no crime can wound,
I fly, pale, undone, and by my shroud haunted,
And fearing to die if I but sleep alone.

TIRED OF THE BITTER REPOSE . . .

Tired of the bitter repose where my idleness hurts
A glory for which I once fled the adorable
Childhood of roses and woods beneath nature's
Azure, and seven times more tired of the harsh
Pact to scoop out every night a fresh grave

Dans le terrain avare et froid de ma cervelle,
Fossoyeur sans pitié pour la stérilité,
— Que dire à cette Aurore, ô Rêves, visité
Par les roses, quand, peur de ses roses livides,
Le vaste cimetière unira les trous vides? —

Je veux délaisser l'Art vorace d'un pays
Cruel, et, souriant aux reproches vieillis
Que me font mes amis, le passé, le génie,
Et ma lampe qui sait pourtant mon agonie,
Imiter le Chinois au cœur limpide et fin
De qui l'extase pure est de peindre la fin
Sur ses tasses de neige à la lune ravie
D'une bizarre fleur qui parfume sa vie
Transparente, la fleur qu'il a sentie, enfant,
Au filigrane bleu de l'âme se greffant.
Et, la mort telle avec le seul rêve du sage,
Serein, je vais choisir un jeune paysage
Que je peindrais encor sur les tasses, distrait.
Une ligne d'azur mince et pâle serait
Un lac, parmi le ciel de porcelaine nue,
Un clair croissant perdu par une blanche nue
Trempe sa corne calme en la glace des eaux,
Non loin de trois grands cils d'émeraude, roseaux.

In the cold and niggard soil of my brain,
Pitiless sexton of sterility,
— What, my Dreams, can I, rose visited, say
To that Dawn when fearful of its livid roses
The vast cemetery joins its hollow graves? —

I would leave the voracious Art of a cruel
Country and smiling at worn-out reproaches
Which my friends and my past and my genius make
And my lamp which natheless my agony knows,
Imitate the Chinese of clear delicate heart
Whose ecstasy pure lies in painting the end,
On his cups as white as moon-ravished snow,
Of a bizarre flower that perfumed his transparent
Life, the flower which he felt as a child
On the filigrane blue of his soul engrafted.
And, my death such with the sage's sole dream,
Some youthful landscape serenely I'll choose
That too will I paint on my cups, abstracted.
A pale and thin line of azure should be
A lake 'mid the heaven of nude porcelain,
A clear crescent moon in a white cloud lost
Dips its calm horn in the icy waters,
Near three great emerald eyelashes, reeds.

BRISE MARINE

La chair est triste, hélas! et j'ai lu tous les livres.
Fuir! là-bas fuir! Je sens que des oiseaux sont ivres
D'être parmi l'écume inconnue et les cieux!
Rien, ni les vieux jardins reflétés par les yeux
Ne retiendra ce cœur qui dans la mer se trempe
O nuits! ni la clarté déserte de ma lampe
Sur le vide papier que la blancheur défend
Et ni la jeune femme allaitant son enfant.
Je partirai! Steamer balançant ta mâture,
Lève l'ancre pour une exotique nature!

Un Ennui, désolé par les cruels espoirs,
Croit encore à l'adieu suprême des mouchoirs!
Et, peut-être, les mâts, invitant les orages
Sont-ils de ceux qu'un vent penche sur les naufrages
Perdus, sans mâts, sans mâts, ni fertiles îlots . . .
Mais, ô mon cœur, entends le chant des matelots!

SEA BREEZE

The flesh is sad alas! and all books I have read.
To fly far away! I know that the sea-birds are drunk
With being amid the unknown foam and the skies!
Nothing, not old gardens reflected in eyes
Will keep back this heart that is plunged in the sea
Oh nights! nor the deserted light of the lamp
On the empty paper which its whiteness protects
Nor even the young woman suckling her child.
I will start! Steamer balancing your masts,
Heave anchor to reach a nature exotic!

Ennui, devastated by my cruel hopes,
Still believes in the handkerchief's final adieu!
And perhaps the masts, inviting tempests,
Are of those which a wind bends over shipwrecks
Lost, without masts, without masts or fertile isles . . .
But oh my heart listen to the sailors' song!

SONNET

(Pour votre chère morte, son ami)

2 *Novembre* 1877

— 'Sur les bois oubliés quand passe l'hiver sombre
Tu te plains, ô captif solitaire du seuil,
Que ce sépulcre à deux qui fera notre orgueil
Hélas! du manque seul des lourds bouquets s'encombre.

Sans écouter Minuit qui jeta son vain nombre,
Une veille t'exalte à ne pas fermer l'œil
Avant que dans les bras de l'ancien fauteuil
Le suprême tison n'ait éclairé mon Ombre.

Qui veut souvent avoir la Visite ne doit
Par trop de fleurs charger la pierre que mon doigt
Soulève avec l'ennui d'une force défunte.

Ame au si clair foyer tremblante de m'asseoir,
Pour revivre il suffit qu'à tes lèvres j'emprunte
Le souffle de mon nom murmuré tout un soir.'

SONNET

(For your dead wife, her friend)

2 November 1877

— 'On the forgotten woods when sombre winter passes
You complain, lonely threshold's prisoner,
That this double sepulchre which is to be our pride
Alone with the lack of great posies is loaded.

Without hearing Midnight cast its vain number,
A vigil exalts you to continue awake
Until in the arms of the old arm-chair
The last fire-glow has illumined my Shade.

He who would oft have the Visitor should not
By too many flowers charge the tomb that my finger
Lifts with the lassitude of a force defunct.

Soul trembling at the so clear hearth to be seated,
To live again it suffices that I borrow from your lips
The breath of my name murmured the evening long.'

DON DU POËME

Je t'apporte l'enfant d'une nuit d'Idumée!
Noire, à l'aile saignante et pâle, déplumée,
Par le verre brûlé d'aromates et d'or,
Par les carreaux glacés, hélas! mornes encor,
L'aurore se jeta sur la lampe angélique.
Palmes! et quand elle a montré cette relique
A ce père essayant un sourire ennemi,
La solitude bleue et stérile a frémi.
O la berceuse, avec ta fille et l'innocence
De vos pieds froids, accueille une horrible naissance
Et ta voix rappelant viole et clavecin,
Avec le doigt fané presseras-tu le sein
Par qui coule en blancheur sibylline la femme
Pour les lèvres que l'air du vierge azur affame?

GIFT OF A POEM

I bring you the child of an Idumaean night!
Black, with wing bleeding, pale and unfeathered,
Through the glass burnt with incense and gold,
Through the panes, frozen, and still gloomy, alas
The dawn burst forth on the lamp angelic,
Palms! and when it had shown this relic
To its father attempting an enemy smile,
The blue and sterile solitude shuddered.
O nursing mother, with your child and the innocence
Of your cold feet, receive this horrible birth
And with your voice recalling viol and clavecin,
With your faded finger, will you press the breast
Whence flows in sibylline whiteness woman
For lips made hungry by the blue virgin air?

HERODIAS

I. SCENE
II. CANTICLE OF ST. JOHN

The French text of Mallarmé's "Overture" to *Hérodiade*, which Roger Fry did not translate, and which, in fact, was not published in France until 1926, will be found in an Appendix on page 304. The *Hérodiade* was first conceived as a verse drama for the stage, and in a letter of 1866 Mallarmé speaks of having completed the "Ouverture musicale" for it. Later (in another letter, in 1896) he writes of the work as consisting of a "Prélude" (which might be the "Overture") *Scène* (which he had published in a magazine in 1869) and a "Finale" (which might be the *Cantique de Saint Jean* — first published posthumously in 1913).

SCÈNE

N. Tu vis! ou vois-je ici l'ombre d'une princesse?
    A mes lèvres tes doigts et leurs bagues et cesse
    De marcher dans un âge ignoré . . .
H.   Reculez.
    Le blond torrent de mes cheveux immaculés
    Quand il baigne mon corps solitaire le glace
    D'horreur, et mes cheveux que la lumière enlace
    Sont immortels. O femme, un baiser me tûrait
    Si la beauté n'était la mort . . .
                                    Par quel attrait
    Menée et quel matin oublié des prophètes
    Verse, sur les lointains mourants, ses tristes fêtes,
    Le sais-je? tu m'as vue, ô nourrice d'hiver,
    Sous la lourde prison de pierres et de fer
    Où de mes vieux lions traînent les siècles fauves
    Entrer, et je marchais, fatale, les mains sauves,
    Dans le parfum désert de ces anciens rois:
    Mais encore as-tu vu quels furent mes effrois?
    Je m'arrête rêvant aux exils, et j'effeuille
    Comme près d'un bassin dont le jet d'eau m'accueille
    Les pâles lys qui sont en moi, tandis qu'épris
    De suivre du regard les languides débris
    Descendre, à travers ma rêverie, en silence,
    Les lions, de ma robe écartent l'indolence

SCENE

NURSE — HERODIAS

N. Alive! Or is it the shadow of a princess I see?
    For my lips your fingers and their rings, and cease
    To walk in an age ignored.
H.   Get back.
    The blonde torrent of my immaculate hair
    Bathing my solitary body, freezes it
    With horror, and my hairs with light entwined
    Are deathless. Woman, a kiss would kill me
    If beauty were not death.
                      By what lure
    Drawn, and what morn forgotten of the prophets
    Pours, on the dying distances, its sad festivity,
    I know not? You have seen me, wintry nurse,
    Down into the heavy prison of iron and stone
    Wherein my aged lions tawny centuries drag
    Enter and walk, fated and hands unscathed,
    Amid the desert perfume of those ancient kings:
    But yet more did you see what were my fears?
    I stop, dreaming of exile and unleaf,
    As by a basin where jetting water invites,
    The pale lilies within me, whilst entranced
    At following with their eyes the languid spoils
    Falling down through my reverie, in silence,
    The lions averting my robe's indolence

Et regardent mes pieds qui calmeraient la mer.
Calme, toi, les frissons de ta sénile chair,
Viens et ma chevelure imitant les manières
Trop farouches qui font votre peur des crinières,
Aide-moi, puisqu'ainsi tu n'oses plus me voir,
À me peigner nonchalamment dans un miroir.

N. Sinon la myrrhe gaie en ses bouteilles closes,
De l'essence ravie aux vieillesses de roses
Voulez-vous, mon enfant, essayer la vertu
Funèbre?

H.   Laisse là ces parfums! ne sais-tu
Que je les hais, nourrice, et veux-tu que je sente
Leur ivresse noyer ma tête languissante?
Je veux que mes cheveux qui ne sont pas des fleurs
A répandre l'oubli des humaines douleurs,
Mais de l'or, à jamais vierge des aromates,
Dans leurs éclairs cruels et dans leurs pâleurs mates,
Observent la froideur stérile du métal,
Vous ayant reflétés, joyaux du mur natal,
Armes, vases depuis ma solitaire enfance.

N. Pardon! l'âge effaçait, reine, votre défense
De mon esprit pâli comme un vieux livre ou noir.

H. Assez! Tiens devant moi ce miroir.

                         O miroir!
Eau froide par l'ennui dans ton cadre gelée
Que de fois et pendant les heures, désolée
Des songes et cherchant mes souvenirs qui sont

Look at my feet which would make calm the sea.
Calm, you, the shudders of your senile flesh
Come, and my tresses imitating the ways
Too wild which make you dread a lion's mane,
Help me, since thus you dare no longer look,
To comb me nonchalantly in the glass.

N. If not gay myrrh in bottles shut,
Of some essence ravished from roses' age
Will you not, child, the virtue essay
Funereal?

H.　　　　Leave there the perfumes! Do you not know
I hate them, nurse, and would you have me feel
Their exaltation drown my languishing head?
I want my hairs, which are not flowers
To spread forgetfulness of human ills,
But gold, for ever virgin of aromatics,
In their cruel lights and matt palenesses
To observe the sterile coldness of metal,
Having reflected you, jewels of my natal walls,
Armour, vases since my lone childhood.

N. Forgive! age had effaced, queen, what you forbade
From my mind grown pale as an old book, or
　　　black . . .

H. Enough, hold up this mirror.
　　　　　　　　　　　Oh mirror!
A cold water frozen with ennui in your frame,
How often, for how long, unvisited
Of dreams, and seeking my remembrances which are

Comme des feuilles sous ta glace au trou profond,
Je m'apparus en toi comme une ombre lointaine,
Mais, horreur! des soirs, dans ta sévère fontaine,
J'ai de mon rêve épars connu la nudité!
Nourrice, suis-je belle?

N.   Un astre, en vérité
Mais cette tresse tombe . . .

H.   Arrête dans ton crime
Qui refroidit mon sang vers sa source, et réprime
Ce geste, impiété fameuse: ah! conte-moi
Quel sûr démon te jette en le sinistre émoi,
Ce baiser, ces parfums offerts et, le dirai-je?
O mon cœur, cette main encore sacrilège,
Car tu voulais, je crois, me toucher, sont un jour
Qui ne finira pas sans malheur sur la tour . . .
O jour qu'Hérodiade avec effroi regarde!

N. Temps bizarre, en effet, de quoi le ciel vous
          garde!
Vous errez, ombre seule et nouvelle fureur,
Et regardant en vous précoce avec terreur:
Mais toujours adorable autant qu'une immortelle,
O mon enfant, et belle affreusement et telle
Que . . .

H.   Mais n'allais-tu pas me toucher?
N.   . . . J'aimerais
Être à qui le destin réserve vos secrets.
H. Oh! tais-toi!
N.   Viendra-t-il parfois?

Like leaves beneath your ice's profoundness
I to myself appeared a far-off shade.
But ah! Some evenings in your severe fount
I of my sparse dreams have known the nudity.
Nurse, am I beautiful?

N.   A star, in truth.
But this tress falls . . .

H.   Stop in your crime
Which chills my blood towards its source, and check
That famously impious gesture: ah! tell me
What sure demon throws on you this sinister spell,
This kiss, these offered scents, and, shall I say it?
My heart, this hand still more sacrilegious,
For I think you would have touched me, make a day
That will not finish without ill on the tower . . .
Oh day, Herodias with dread looks upon!

N. Strange times, indeed, from which heaven protect
    you!
You wander, solitary shade, and a new fierceness,
And look within, precocious with dread:
But always adorable like an immortal,
O my child, and beautiful, terribly, and such
That . . .

H.   But were you not going to touch me?

N.   . . . I should love
To be for whom Destiny guards your secrets.

H. Oh! Silence!

N.   Will he ever come?

H.   Étoiles pures,
   N'entendez pas!

N.   Comment, sinon parmi d'obscures
   Épouvantes, songer plus implacable encor
   Et comme suppliant le dieu que le trésor
   De votre grâce attend! et pour qui, dévorée
   D'angoisses, gardez-vous la splendeur ignorée
   Et le mystère vain de votre être?

H.   Pour moi.

N. Triste fleur qui croît seule et n'a pas d'autre émoi
   Que son sombre dans l'eau vue avec atonie.

H. Va, garde ta pitié comme ton ironie.

N. Toutefois expliquez: oh! non, naïve enfant,
   Décroîtra, quelque jour, ce dédain triomphant . . .

H. Mais qui me toucherait, des lions respectée?
   Du reste, je ne veux rien d'humain et, sculptée,
   Si tu me vois les yeux perdus au paradis,
   C'est quand je me souviens de ton lait bu jadis.

N. Victime lamentable à son destin offerte!

H. Oui, c'est pour moi, pour moi, que je fleuris, déserte!
   Vous le savez, jardins d'améthyste, enfouis
   Sans fin dans de savants abîmes éblouis,
   Ors ignorés, gardant votre antique lumière
   Sous le sombre sommeil d'une terre première,
   Vous pierres où mes yeux comme de purs bijoux
   Empruntent leur clarté mélodieuse, et vous
   Métaux qui donnez à ma jeune chevelure
   Une splendeur fatale et sa massive allure!

H.   Pure stars,
   Hear not!
N.   How, if not amid obscure
   Alarms, to dream more implacable still
   And as a suppliant the god whom the treasure
   Of your grace awaits! For whom, devoured
   By anxiety keep you the splendour ignored
   And the vain mystery of your being?
H.   For myself.
N. Sad flower which grows alone and has no other joy
   Than its own image seen in water listlessly.
H. Go, keep your pity as your irony.
N. Only explain: Oh! no, naive child,
   It must grow less one day, this triumphant disdain.
H. But who would touch me, of the lions untouched?
   Besides, I want naught human, and if sculptured
   You see me with eyes lost in Paradise
   'Tis when I bring to mind your milk once drunk.
N. Ah! Lamentable victim offered to its fate!
H. Yes, it's for me, for me that I flower, deserted!
   You know it, gardens of amethyst, hid
   Endlessly in cunning abysses and dazzled,
   Ignored gold, keeping your antique light
   Under the sombre sleep of a primæval soil,
   You stones whence my eyes like pure jewels
   Borrow their melodious brightness, and you
   Metals which give my youthful tresses
   A fatal splendour and their massive sway!

69

Quant à toi, femme née en des siècles malins
Pour la méchanceté des antres sibyllins,
Qui parles d'un mortel! selon qui, des calices
De mes robes, arôme aux farouches délices,
Sortirait le frisson blanc de ma nudité,
Prophétise que si le tiède azur d'été,
Vers lui nativement la femme se dévoile,
Me voit dans ma pudeur grelottante d'étoile,
Je meurs!

                J'aime l'horreur d'être vierge et je veux
Vivre parmi l'effroi que me font mes cheveux
Pour, le soir, retirée en ma couche, reptile
Inviolé sentir en la chair inutile
Le froid scintillement de ta pâle clarté
Toi qui te meurs, toi qui brûles de chasteté,
Nuit blanche de glaçons et de neige cruelle!

Et ta sœur solitaire, ô ma sœur éternelle
Mon rêve montera vers toi: telle déjà
Rare limpidité d'un cœur qui le songea,
Je me crois seule en ma monotone patrie
Et tout, autour de moi, vit dans l'idolâtrie
D'un mirror qui reflète en son calme dormant
Hérodiade au clair regard de diamant . . .
O charme dernier, oui! je le sens, je suis seule.
N. Madame, allez-vous donc mourir?

For you, woman, born in an evil age
As for the mischief of sibylline caves,
Who talk of a mortal! who declare, from the calyx
Of my robes, aromatic of fierce delights,
There should issue the white shudder of my nudity,
Prophesy too that if the warm blue of summer,
Towards which natively woman unveils,
Sees me in my pudour a shivering star,
I die!

I love virginity's horror, and I would
Live in the terror that my locks inspire
So, at evening, drawn back in my couch, a reptile
Inviolate, to feel in my purposeless flesh
The cold scintillations of your pale light
You, who die to yourself, you, who burn with chas-
    tity,
White night of ice-clots and cruel snow!

And your lonely sister, oh my sister eternal
My dream will mount you-wards: such already
Rare limpidity of a heart which dreamed it,
I think myself alone in my monotonous country
And, around me, all lives in the idolatry
Of a mirror, reflecting in its sleeping calm
Herodias of the clear diamond look . . .
Oh! supreme joy, yes, I know it, I am alone.
N. Madam, are you to die thus?

H.   Non, pauvre aïeule,
Sois calme et, t'éloignant, pardonne à ce cœur dur
Mais avant, si tu veux, clos les volets, l'azur
Séraphique sourit dans les vitres profondes,
Et je déteste, moi, le bel azur!

                          Des ondes
Se bercent et, là-bas, sais-tu pas un pays
Où le sinistre ciel ait les regards haïs
De Vénus qui, le soir, brûle dans le feuillage;
J'y partirais.

                 Allume encore, enfantillage
Dis-tu, ces flambeaux où la cire au feu léger
Pleure parmi l'or vain quelque pleur étranger
Et . . .
N.   Maintenant?
H.   Adieu.
                Vous mentez, ô fleur nue
De mes lèvres!
           J'attends une chose inconnue
Ou peut-être, ignorant le mystère et vos cris,
Jetez-vous les sanglots suprêmes et meurtris
D'une enfance sentant parmi les rêveries
Se séparer enfin ses froides pierreries.

H.   No, my poor grandam,
Be calm, and withdrawing, pardon this hard heart,
But first, if you will, close the shutters, the azure
Seraphic smiles in the profound panes,
And I detest, I, the beautiful azure!

                                        Waves
Rock gently and, yonder, know you not a land
Where the sinister sky has the hated looks
Of Venus who, the eve long, burns in the leafage;
I'll thither.

                Light, too, it's childish
You'll say, those torches where wax with subtle fire
Weeps mid the vain gold some strange tear
And . . .
N.   And now?
H.   Adieu.
                        You lie, naked flower
Of my lips!
                        I await a thing unknown
Or perhaps, ignoring the mystery and your cries,
You utter the ultimate, bruised, sobs
Of a childhood feeling amid its reveries
Separate each from each its cold polished stones.

CANTIQUE DE SAINT JEAN

Le soleil que sa halte
Surnaturelle exalte
Aussitôt redescend
   Incandescent

Je sens comme aux vertèbres
S'éployer des ténèbres
Toutes dans un frisson
   A l'unisson

Et ma tête surgie
Solitaire vigie
Dans les vols triomphaux
   De cette faux

Comme rupture franche
Plutôt refoule ou tranche
Les anciens désaccords
   Avec le corps

Qu'elle de jeûnes ivre
S'opiniâtre à suivre
En quelque bond hagard
   Son pur regard

CANTICLE OF ST. JOHN

The sun whose stay on high
Is supernatural
As soon descends again
   Incandescent

I feel as in my spine
Darknesses spreading
All shivering
   In unison

And my head aris'n
In solitary watch
'Mid the triumphal flights
   Of ah! this scythe

As a rupture clean
Rather keeps back or cuts
Its ancient disaccords
   With the body's flesh

Let *it* with fasting drunk
Follow obstinately
With haggard leap
   Its pure regard

Là-haut où la froidure
Éternelle n'endure
Que vous le surpassiez
   Tous ô glaciers

Mais selon un baptême
Illuminée au même
Principe qui m'élut
   Penche un salut.

Up thither where the cold
Eternal not endures
That you should it surpass
    Oh glaciers all.

But by a baptism
Illumined by the same
Principle which chose me
    Bows a salute.

THE AFTERNOON OF A FAUN

ECLOGUE

LE FAUNE

Ces nymphes, je les veux perpétuer.

                                    Si clair,
Leur incarnat léger, qu'il voltige dans l'air
Assoupi de sommeils touffus.

                              Aimai-je un rêve?
Mon doute, amas de nuit ancienne, s'achève
En maint rameau subtil, qui, demeuré les vrais
Bois mêmes, prouve, hélas! que bien seul je m'offrais
Pour triomphe la faute idéale de roses.
Réfléchissons . . .

                        ou si les femmes dont tu gloses
Figurent un souhait de tes sens fabuleux!
Faune, l'illusion s'échappe des yeux bleus
Et froids, comme une source en pleurs, de la plus chaste:
Mais, l'autre tout soupirs, dis-tu qu'elle contraste
Comme brise du jour chaude dans ta toison!
Que non! par l'immobile et lasse pâmoison
Suffoquant de chaleurs le matin frais s'il lutte,
Ne murmure point d'eau que ne verse ma flûte
Au bosquet arrosé d'accords; et le seul vent
Hors des deux tuyaux prompt à s'exhaler avant

THE FAUN

These nymphs I would perpetuate.

                              So clear
Their light carnation, that it floats in the air
Heavy with tufted slumbers.

                    Was it a dream I loved?
My doubt, a heap of ancient night, is finishing
In many a subtle branch, which, left the true
Wood itself, proves, alas! that all alone I gave
Myself for triumph the ideal sin of roses.
Let me reflect. . . .

                    if the girls of which you tell
Figure a wish of your fabulous senses!
Faun, the illusion escapes from the blue eyes
And cold, like a spring in tears, of the chaster one:
But, the other, all sighs, do you say she contrasts
Like a breeze of hot day in your fleece!
But no! through the still, weary faintness
Choking with heat the fresh morn if it strives,
No water murmurs but what my flute pours
On the chord sprinkled thicket; and the sole wind
Prompt to exhale from my two pipes, before

Qu'il disperse le son dans une pluie aride,
C'est, à l'horizon pas remué d'une ride,
Le visible et serein souffle artificiel
De l'inspiration, qui regagne le ciel.

O bords siciliens d'un calme marécage
Qu'à l'envi de soleils ma vanité saccage,
Tacite sous les fleurs d'étincelles, CONTEZ
'Que je coupais ici les creux roseaux domptés
Par le talent; quand, sur l'or glauque de lointaines
Verdures dédiant leur vigne à des fontaines,
Ondoie une blancheur animale au repos:
Et qu'au prélude lent où naissent les pipeaux
Ce vol de cygnes, non! de naïades se sauve
Ou plonge . . .'

                 Inerte, tout brûle dans l'heure fauve
Sans marquer par quel art ensemble détala
Trop d'hymen souhaité de qui cherche le *la*:
Alors m'éveillerai-je à la ferveur première,
Droit et seul, sous un flot antique de lumière,
Lys! et l'un de vous tous pour l'ingénuité.

Autre que ce doux rien par leur lèvre ébruité,
Le baiser, qui tout bas des perfides assure,
Mon sein, vierge de preuve, atteste une morsure
Mystérieuse, due à quelque auguste dent;

It scatters the sound in a waterless shower,
Is, on the horizon's unwrinkled space,
The visible serene artificial breath
Of th'inspiration, which regains the sky.

Oh you, Sicilian shores of a calm marsh
That more than the suns my vanity havocs,
Silent beneath the flowers of sparks, RELATE
'That here I was cutting the hollow reeds tamed
By talent, when on the dull gold of the distant
Verdures dedicating their vines to the springs,
There waves an animal whiteness at rest:
And that to the prelude where the pipes first stir
This flight of swans, no! Naiads, flies
Or plunges . . .'

                      Inert, all burns in the fierce hour
Nor marks by what art all at once bolted
Too much hymen desired by who seeks the *la:*
Then shall I awake to the primitive fervour,
Straight and alone, 'neath antique floods of light,
Lilies! and one of you all through my ingenuousness.

As well as this sweet nothing their lips purr,
The kiss, which a hush assures of the perfid ones,
My breast, though proofless, still attests a bite
Mysterious, due to some august tooth;

Mais, bast! arcane tel élut pour confident
Le jonc vaste et jumeau dont sous l'azur on joue:
Qui, détournant à soi le trouble de la joue
Rêve, dans un solo long, que nous amusions
La beauté d'alentour par des confusions
Fausses entre elle-même et notre chant crédule;
Et de faire aussi haut que l'amour se module
Évanouir du songe ordinaire de dos
Ou de flanc pur suivis avec mes regards clos,
Une sonore, vaine et monotone ligne.

Tâche donc, instrument des fuites, ô maligne
Syrinx, de refleurir aux lacs où tu m'attends!
Moi, de ma rumeur fier, je vais parler longtemps
Des déesses; et par d'idolâtres peintures,
A leur ombre enlever encore des ceintures:
Ainsi, quand des raisins j'ai sucé la clarté,
Pour bannir un regret par ma feinte écarté,
Rieur, j'élève au ciel d'été la grappe vide
Et, soufflant dans ses peaux lumineuses, avide
D'ivresse, jusqu'au soir je regarde au travers.

O nymphes, regonflons des SOUVENIRS divers.
'Mon œil, trouant les joncs, dardait chaque encolure
Immortelle, qui noie en l'onde sa brûlure
Avec un cri de rage au ciel de la forêt;
Et le splendide bain de cheveux disparaît
Dans les clartés et les frissons, ô pierreries!

But enough! for confidant such mystery chose
The great double reed which one plays 'neath the blue:
Which, the cheek's trouble turning to itself
Dreams, in a solo long, we might amuse
Surrounding beauties by confusions false
Between themselves and our credulous song;
And to make, just as high as love modulates,
Die out of the everyday dream of a back
Or a pure flank followed by my curtained eyes,
An empty, sonorous, monotonous line.

Try then, instrument of flights, oh malign
Syrinx, to reflower by the lakes where you wait for me!
I, proud of my rumour, for long I will talk
Of goddesses; and by picturings idolatrous,
From their shades unloose yet more of their girdles:
So when of grapes the clearness I've sucked,
To banish regret by my ruse disavowed,
Laughing, I lift the empty bunch to the sky,
Blowing into its luminous skins and athirst
To be drunk, till the evening I keep looking through.

Oh nymphs, we diverse MEMORIES refill.
'My eye, piercing the reeds, shot at each immortal
Neck, which drowned its burning in the wave
With a cry of rage to the forest sky;
And the splendid bath of their hair disappears
In the shimmer and shuddering, oh diamonds!

85

J'accours; quand, à mes pieds, s'entrejoignent (meur-
    tries
De la langueur goûtée à ce mal d'être deux)
Des dormeuses parmi leurs seuls bras hasardeux;
Je les ravis, sans les désenlacer, et vole
A ce massif, haï par l'ombrage frivole,
De roses tarissant tout parfum au soleil,
Où notre ébat au jour consumé soit pareil.'
Je t'adore, courroux des vierges, ô délice
Farouche du sacré fardeau nu qui se glisse
Pour fuir ma lèvre en feu buvant, comme **un éclair**
Tressaille! la frayeur secrète de la chair:
Des pieds de l'inhumaine au cœur de la timide
Que délaisse à la fois une innocence, humide
De larmes folles ou de moins tristes vapeurs.
'Mon crime, c'est d'avoir, gai de vaincre ces peurs
Traîtresses, divisé la touffe échevelée
De baisers que les dieux gardaient si bien mêlée;
Car, à peine j'allais cacher un rire ardent
Sous les replis heureux d'une seule (gardant
Par un doigt simple, afin que sa candeur de **plume**
Se teignît a l'émoi de sa sœur qui s'allume,
La petite, naïve et ne rougissant pas:)
Que de mes bras, défaits par de vagues trépas,
Cette proie, à jamais ingrate se délivre
Sans pitié du sanglot dont j'étais encore ivre.'

I run, when, there at my feet, enlaced, lie
(Hurt by the languor they taste to be two)
Girls sleeping amid their own casual arms;
Them I seize, and not disentangling them, fly
To this thicket, hated by the frivolous shade,
Of roses drying up their scent in the sun
Where our delight may be like the day sun-consumed.'
I adore it, the anger of virgins, the wild
Delight of the sacred nude burden which slips
To escape from my hot lips drinking, as lightning
Flashes! the secret terror of the flesh:
From the feet of the cruel one to the heart of the timid
Who together lose an innocence, humid
With wild tears or less sorrowful vapours.
'My crime is that I, gay at conquering the treacherous
Fears, the dishevelled tangle divided
Of kisses, the gods kept so well commingled;
For before I could stifle my fiery laughter
In the happy recesses of one (while I kept
With a finger alone, that her feathery whiteness
Should be dyed by her sister's kindling desire,
The younger one, naive and without a blush)
When from my arms, undone by vague failing,
This prey without gratitude sets herself free
Nor pities the sob wherewith I was still drunk.'

Tant pis! vers le bonheur d'autres m'entraîneront
Par leur tresse nouée aux cornes de mon front:
Tu sais, ma passion, que, pourpre et déjà mûre,
Chaque grenade éclate et d'abeilles murmure;
Et notre sang, épris de qui le va saisir,
Coule pour tout l'essaim éternel du désir.
A l'heure où ce bois d'or et de cendres se teinte
Une fête s'exalte en la feuillée éteinte:
Etna! c'est parmi toi visité de Vénus
Sur ta lave posant ses talons ingénus,
Quand tonne un somme triste ou s'épuise la flamme.
Je tiens la reine!

                    O sûr châtiment . . .

                                        Non, mais l'âme
De paroles vacante et ce corps alourdi
Tard succombent au fier silence de midi:
Sans plus il faut dormir en l'oubli du blasphème,
Sur le sable altéré gisant et comme j'aime
Ouvrir ma bouche à l'astre efficace des vins!

Couple, adieu; je vais voir l'ombre que tu devins.

Ah well, towards happiness others will lead me
With their tresses knotted to the horns of my brow:
You know, my passion, that purple and just ripe,
The pomegranates burst and murmur with bees;
And our blood, aflame for her who will take it,
Flows for all the eternal swarm of desire.
At the hour when this wood's dyed with gold and with
    ashes
A festival glows in the leafage extinguished:
Etna! 'tis amid you, visited by Venus
On your lava fields placing her candid feet,
When a sad stillness thunders wherein the flame dies.
I hold the queen!

        O penalty sure . . .

                No, but the soul
Void of word and my body weighed down
Succumb in the end to midday's proud silence:
No more, I must sleep, forgetting the outrage,
On the thirsty sand lying, and as I delight
Open my mouth to wine's potent star!

Adieu, both! I shall see the shade you became.

SAINTE

A la fenêtre recélant
Le santal vieux qui se dédore
De sa viole étincelant
Jadis avec flûte ou mandore,

Est la Sainte pâle, étalant
Le livre vieux qui se déplie
Du Magnificat ruisselant
Jadis selon vêpre et complie:

A ce vitrage d'ostensoir
Que frôle une harpe par l'Ange
Formée avec son vol du soir
Pour la délicate phalange

Du doigt que, sans le vieux santal
Ni le vieux livre, elle balance
Sur le plumage instrumental,
Musicienne du silence.

SAINT

At the window holding
The old cedarwood disgilt
Of her lute shining
Once with flute or mandola,

Stands the pale saint spreading
The old book which unfolds
On the Magnificat glistening
Once for vespers and compline:

At this monstrance window
Brushed by the harp that an angel
Makes in his evening flight
For the delicate tip

Of the finger that without cedar
Or old book she balances
On the feathered instrument,
Musician of silence.

TOAST FUNÈBRE

O de notre bonheur, toi, le fatal emblème!

Salut de la démence et libation blême,
Ne crois pas qu'au magique espoir du corridor
J'offre ma coupe vide où souffre un monstre d'or!
Ton apparition ne va pas me suffire:
Car je t'ai mis, moi-même, en un lieu de porphyre.
Le rite est pour les mains d'éteindre le flambeau
Contre le fer épais des portes du tombeau:
Et l'on ignore mal, élu pour notre fête
Très simple de chanter l'absence du poëte,
Que ce beau monument l'enferme tout entier:
Si ce n'est que la gloire ardente du métier,
Jusqu'à l'heure commune et vile de la cendre,
Par le carreau qu'allume un soir fier d'y descendre,
Retourne vers les feux du pur soleil mortel!

Magnifique, total et solitaire, tel
Tremble de s'exhaler le faux orgueil des hommes.
Cette foule hagarde! elle annonce: Nous sommes
La triste opacité de nos spectres futurs.
Mais le blason des deuils épars sur de vains murs
J'ai méprisé l'horreur lucide d'une larme,
Quand, sourd même à mon vers sacré qui ne l'alarme
Quelqu'un de ces passants, fier, aveugle et muet,
Hôte de son linceul vague, se transmuait

A FUNERAL TOAST

Oh of our happiness, Thou, the fatal emblem!

A health to madness and a blank libation,
Think not to the corridor's magic hope
I offer my empty cup where suffers a monster of gold!
Your apparition is not enough for me:
For I have put you, myself, into a porphyry chamber.
The rite is now for our hands to put out the torch
Against the thick iron of the tomb's portal:
Nor am I ignorant, elected for our simple
Feast that is to sing the absence of the poet,
That this fair monument contains him altogether;
Unless it be that the ardent glory of this craft,
Until the common hour and vile brings all to dust,
By the pane lit by an evening proud to discard there
Returns towards the fires of our pure mortal sun!

Magnificent, total and solitary, such
The false pride of men trembles to declare itself.
This haggard crowd makes claim: 'We are
The sad opacity of our future spectres.'
But, blazon of mourning scattered on vain walls,
I treated with scorn the tears' lucid horror,
When, deaf to my sacred verse which he fears not,
One of these passers-by, proud, blind and speechless,
Guest of his own vague shroud, was transmuted

En le vierge héros de l'attente posthume.
Vaste gouffre apporté dans l'amas de la brume
Par l'irascible vent des mots qu'il n'a pas dits,
Le néant à cet Homme aboli de jadis:
'Souvenirs d'horizons, qu'est-ce, ô toi, que la Terre?'
Hurle ce songe; et, voix dont la clarté s'altère,
L'espace a pour jouet le cri: 'Je ne sais pas!'

Le Maître, par un œil profond, a, sur ses pas,
Apaisé de l'éden l'inquiète merveille
Dont le frisson final, dans sa voix seule, éveille
Pour la Rose et le Lys le mystère d'un nom.
Est-il de ce destin rien qui demeure, non?
O vous tous, oubliez une croyance sombre.
Le splendide génie éternel n'a pas d'ombre.
Moi, de votre désir soucieux, je veux voir,
A qui s'évanouit, hier, dans le devoir
Idéal que nous font les jardins de cet astre,
Survivre pour l'honneur du tranquille désastre
Une agitation solennelle par l'air
De paroles, pourpre ivre et grand calice clair,
Que, pluie et diamant, le regard diaphane
Resté là sur ces fleurs dont nulle ne se fane,
Isole parmi l'heure et le rayon du jour!

C'est de nos vrais bosquets déjà tout le séjour,
Où le poëte pur a pour geste humble et large
De l'interdire au rêve, ennemi de sa charge:

94

Into the virgin hero of the posthumous hope.
Vast gulf brought about in the misty mass
By the irascible wind of his words unuttered,
Nothingness to this man who has ceased:
'Memories of horizons, what, I ask you, is the Earth?'
Yells this dream, and, voice whose clarity's fading,
Space gets for plaything the cry: 'I know not'!

The Master, by his deep eye, has, as he went,
Appeased the disquieting marvel of Eden
Of which the last quiver, in his voice, awakes
For the Rose and the Lily the mystery of a name.
Does nothing endure then of this destiny, no?
Oh forget, all of you, so sombre a creed.
The splendid eternal genius is without shade.
I, careful of your desire, I hope to see
Him who, yesterday, vanished in the ideal
Duty imposed by the gardens of this star,
Survived for the honour of the calm disaster
By a solemn agitation in the air of words,
Ebrious purple and great clear chalice,
Which, rain and diamonds, his diaphanous look
[Remaining] there on the flowers of which none fades,
Isolates in the hour and the days luminosity!

'Tis of our true boscage already the sojourn
Where the pure poet by his humble grand gesture
Must keep out the dream, enemy of his charge;

Afin que le matin de son repos altier,
Quand la mort ancienne est comme pour Gautier
De n'ouvrir pas les yeux sacrés et de se taire,
Surgisse, de l'allée ornement tributaire,
Le sépulcre solide où gît tout ce qui nuit,
Et l'avare silence et la massive nuit.

AUTRE ÉVENTAIL

de Mademoiselle Mallarmé

O rêveuse, pour que je plonge
Au pur délice sans chemin,
Sache, par un subtil mensonge,
Garder mon aile dans ta main.

Une fraîcheur de crépuscule
Te vient à chaque battement
Dont le coup prisonnier recule
L'horizon délicatement.

Vertige! voici que frissonne
L'espace comme un grand baiser
Qui, fou de naître pour personne
Ne peut jaillir ni s'apaiser.

So that the morning of his high repose,
When ancient death is, as for Gautier now,
The sacred eyes to close and to be silent,
There may arise, tributary ornament of the alley,
The solid tomb where lies all that can harm,
Both grudging silence and oppressive night.

ANOTHER FAN

Belonging to Mademoiselle Mallarmé

Dear dreamer, that I may plunge
Into pure, trackless delight,
Know, by a subtle deceit,
How to hold my wing in your hand.

A freshness of twilight comes
Upon you at each wing-beat
Whose prisoned strokes defer
The horizon delicately.

Vastness! See how thrills
Space like an immense kiss
Which, mad to be born for no one
Neither can flow nor be still.

Sens-tu le paradis farouche
Ainsi qu'un rire enseveli
Se couler du coin de ta bouche
Au fond de l'unanime pli!

Le sceptre des rivages roses
Stagnants sur les soirs d'or, ce l'est,
Ce blanc vol fermé que tu poses
Contre le feu d'un bracelet.

PETIT AIR

Quelconque une solitude
Sans le cygne ni le quai
Mire sa désuétude
Au regard que j'abdiquai

Ici de la gloriole
Haute à ne la pas toucher
Dont maint ciel se bariole
Avec les ors de coucher

Mais langoureusement longe
Comme de blanc linge ôté
Tel fugace oiseau si plonge
Exultatrice à côté

Dans l'onde toi devenue
Ta jubilation nue.

98

Do you feel the wild paradise
Which like laughter entombed
Flows from the lips' last curve
Down the unanimous fold!

The sceptre of rose-red shores
Stagnant on evenings of gold is
This white flight which you place
Against a bracelet's fire.

LITTLE AIR

Just a solitude
Without the swan and quay
Mirrors its loneliness
In the look which I turned

Here from the glitter
Too high to touch
In which the sky's streaked
With sunset golds

But languidly coasts
Like white linen doffed
Some shy bird if plunges
Exulting beside

In the billow become you
Your nude jubilation.

99

SONNET

Quand l'ombre menaça de la fatale loi
Tel vieux Rêve, désir et mal de mes vertèbres,
Affligé de périr sous les plafonds funèbres
Il a ployé son aile indubitable en moi.

Luxe, ô salle d'ébène où, pour séduire un roi
Se tordent dans leur mort des guirlandes célèbres,
Vous n'êtes qu'un orgueil menti par les ténèbres
Aux yeux du solitaire ébloui de sa foi.

Oui, je sais qu'au lointain de cette nuit, la Terre
Jette d'un grand éclat l'insolite mystère
Sous les siècles hideux qui l'obscurcissent moins.

L'espace à soi pareil qu'il s'accroisse ou se nie
Roule dans cet ennui des feux vils pour témoins
Que s'est d'un astre en fête allumé le génie.

SONNET

When the shadow menaced with its fatal law
Some ancient Dream, my spine's desire and ill,
Afflicted at perishing beneath the funereal ceiling
It has folded in me its indubitable wing.

Luxury! Ebony hall where, to flatter a king
There twist in their death the famous garlands,
You are nought but a pride lied by the darkness
To the eyes of the solitary dazzled by his faith.

Yes, I know that in this night's ultimate distance
The Earth sheds the glow of a rare mystery
And the hideous centuries obscure it less.

Space like to itself let it grow or grow less
Rolls 'mid this ennui vile fires for witness
That of a star at festival the genius is lit.

SONNET

Le vierge, le vivace et le bel aujourd'hui
Va-t-il nous déchirer avec un coup d'aile ivre
Ce lac dur oublié que hante sous le givre
Le transparent glacier des vols qui n'ont pas fui!

Un cygne d'autrefois se souvient que c'est lui
Magnifique mais qui sans espoir se délivre
Pour n'avoir pas chanté la région où vivre
Quand du stérile hiver a resplendi l'ennui.

Tout son col secouera cette blanche agonie
Par l'espace infligée à l'oiseau qui le nie,
Mais non l'horreur du sol où le plumage est pris.

Fantôme qu'à ce lieu son pur éclat assigne,
Il s'immobilise au songe froid de mépris
Que vêt parmi l'exil inutile le Cygne.

SONNET

Victorieusement fui le suicide beau
Tison de gloire, sang par écume, or, tempête!
O rire si là-bas une pourpre s'apprête
A ne tendre royal que mon absent tombeau.

SONNET

This virgin, beautiful and lively day
Will it tear with a stroke of its drunken wing
The hard, forgotten lake which haunts 'neath the frost
The transparent glacier of flights unflown!

A swan of past days recalls it is he
Magnificent but without hope who is freed
For not having sung the realm where to live
When sterile winter's ennui has shone forth.

All his neck will shake off this white agony
By space inflicted on the bird who denies it,
But not the horror of the soil where his plumage is
        caught.

Fantom that to this place his brightness assigns him,
He is stilled in the icy dream of contempt
Which clothes in his useless exile the Swan.

SONNET

Victoriously fled is the grand suicide
Glow of glory, blood in foam, tempest and gold.
Ah, ha! if down there a purple is spread
To pall royally my absence of tomb.

Quoi! de tout cet éclat pas même le lambeau
S'attarde, il est minuit, à l'ombre qui nous fête
Excepté qu'un trésor présomptueux de tête
Verse son caressé nonchaloir sans flambeau,

La tienne si toujours le délice! la tienne
Oui seule qui du ciel évanoui retienne
Un peu de puéril triomphe en t'en coiffant

Avec clarté quand sur les coussins tu la poses
Comme un casque guerrier d'impératrice enfant
Dont pour te figurer il tomberait des roses.

SONNET

Ses purs ongles très haut dédiant leur onyx,
L'Angoisse, ce minuit, soutient, lampadophore,
Maint rêve vespéral brûlé par le Phénix
Que ne recueille pas de cinéraire amphore

Sur les crédences, au salon vide: nul ptyx,
Aboli bibelot d'inanité sonore
(Car le Maître est allé puiser des pleurs au Styx
Avec ce seul objet dont le Néant s'honore.)

Mais proche la croisée au nord vacante, un or
Agonise selon peut-être le décor
Des licornes ruant du feu contre une nixe,

What! of all that splendour not even a shred
Lingers on, it is midnight, in our festival shade
Except that presumptuous treasure of head
Which pours without torch its languor caressed,

Yours! so ever delightful, ah yours!
Which alone of the sky that is vanished retains
What with puerile triumph you wind in your hair

Shining when on your cushion it lies
Like the warrior casque of an empress child
Whence, to figure yourself, roses should pour.

SONNET

Her pure nails very high dedicating their onyx,
Anguish, this midnight, upholds, the lampbearer,
Many vesperal dreams by the Phenix burnt
That are not gathered up in the funeral urn

On the credences, in the empty room: no ptyx,
Abolished bibelot of sounding inanity
(For the Master is gone to draw tears from the Styx
With this sole object which Nothingness honours.)

But near the window void Northwards, a gold
Dies down composing perhaps a decor
Of unicorns kicking sparks at a nixey,

Elle, défunte nue en le miroir, encor
Que, dans l'oubli fermé par le cadre, se fixe
De scintillations sitôt le septuor.

LA CHEVELURE . . .

La chevelure vol d'une flamme à l'extrême
Occident de désirs pour la tout déployer
Se pose (je dirais mourir un diadème)
Vers le front couronné son ancien foyer

Mais sans or soupirer que cette vive nue
L'ignition du feu toujours intérieur
Originellement la seule continue
Dans le joyau de l'œil véridique ou rieur

Une nudité de héros tendre diffame
Celle qui ne mouvant astre ni feux au doigt
Rien qu'à simplifier avec gloire la femme
Accomplit par son chef fulgurante l'exploit

De semer de rubis le doute qu'elle écorche
Ainsi qu'une joyeuse et tutélaire torche.

She, nude and defunct in the mirror, while yet,
In the oblivion closed by the frame there appears
Of scintillations at once the septet.

THE MASS OF HAIR . . .

The mass of hair a flame's flight to the extreme
Occident of desires there to unfold all
Settles (call it the dying of a diadem)
Towards the crowned brow its ancient hearth

But deprived of gold to sigh that this live cloud
The ignition of a fire always internal
Originally the only one should continue
In the jewel of the eye serious or mocking

A nakedness of a tender hero defames
That which nor moving star nor fire on the finger
Nought but simplifying the woman with glory
Accomplishes by its head flaming the exploit

Of sowing with rubies the doubt it has grazed
As might a joyous and tutelary torch.

LE TOMBEAU D'EDGAR POE

Tel qu'en Lui-même enfin l'éternité le change,
Le Poëte suscite avec un glaive nu
Son siècle épouvanté de n'avoir pas connu
Que la mort triomphait dans cette voix étrange!

Eux, comme un vil sursaut d'hydre oyant jadis l'ange
Donner un sens plus pur aux mots de la tribu
Proclamèrent très haut le sortilège bu
Dans le flot sans honneur de quelque noir mélange.

Du sol et de la nue hostiles, ô grief!
Si notre idée avec ne sculpte un bas-relief
Dont la tombe de Poe éblouissante s'orne

Calme bloc ici-bas chu d'un désastre obscur
Que ce granit du moins montre à jamais sa borne
Aux noirs vols du Blasphème épars dans le futur.

LE TOMBEAU DE CHARLES BAUDELAIRE

Le temple enseveli divulgue par la bouche
Sépulcrale d'égout bavant boue et rubis
Abominablement quelque idole Anubis
Tout le museau flambé comme un aboi farouche

THE TOMB OF EDGAR POE

Such as to himself eternity's changed him,
The Poet arouses with his naked sword
His age fright-stricken for not having known
That Death was triumphing in that strange voice!

They, with a Hydra's vile spasm at hearing the angel
Giving a sense more pure to the words of their tribe
Proclaimed aloud the sortilege drunk
In the dishonoured flow of some black brew.

Oh, Grief! From soil and from the hostile cloud,
If thence our idea cannot carve a relief
Wherewith to adorn Poe's shining tomb

Calm block fallen down here from some dark disaster
May this granite at least show forever their bourn
To the black flights of Blasphemy sparse in the future.

THE TOMB OF CHARLES BAUDELAIRE

The buried temple divulges by its drain's
Sepulchral mouth slobbering mud and rubies
Abominably some idol of Anubis
All its muzzle aflame with wild barking

Ou que le gaz récent torde la mèche louche
Essuyeuse on le sait des opprobres subis
Il allume hagard un immortel pubis
Dont le vol selon le réverbère découche

Quel feuillage séché dans les cités sans soir
Votif pourra bénir comme elle se rasseoir
Contre le marbre vainement de Baudelaire

Au voile qui la ceint absente avec frissons
Celle son Ombre même un poison tutélaire
Toujours à respirer si nous en périssons.

TOMBEAU

Anniversaire — Janvier 1897

Le noir roc courroucé que la bise le roule
Ne s'arrêtera ni sous de pieuses mains
Tâtant sa ressemblance avec les maux humains
Comme pour en bénir quelque funeste moule.

Ici presque toujours si le ramier roucoule
Cet immatériel deuil opprime de maints
Nubiles plis l'astre mûri des lendemains
Dont un scintillement argentera la foule.

Or if the recent gas twists the foul wick
That gathers, one knows, the insults endured
It lights a strange, immortal pubis
Whose flight persists though the lantern swings

What foliage dried in eveningless cities
Votive could bless as his shade could sit
Vainly against Baudelaire's marble

With the shivering veil that clothes its absence
It, his shade, like a tutelary poison
Always to be breathed even if we die of it.

TOMB

Anniversary — January 1897

The black rock angry that the wind rolls it
Will not be stayed even by pious hands
Seeking its likeness to all human ills
As though to bless thereof some tragic mould.

Here almost always if the ring-dove coos
This immaterial mourning imprints many
Nubile folds on the future's ripened star
Whose glittering will silver o'er the crowd

Qui cherche, parcourant le solitaire bond
Tantôt extérieur de notre vagabond —
Verlaine? Il est caché parmi l'herbe, Verlaine

A ne surprendre que naïvement d'accord
La lèvre sans y boire ou tarir son haleine
Un peu profond ruisseau calomnié la mort.

TOUTE L'ÂME RÉSUMÉE . . .

Toute l'âme résumée
Quand lente nous l'expirons
Dans plusieurs ronds de fumée
Abolis en autres ronds

Atteste quelque cigare
Brûlant savamment pour peu
Que la cendre se sépare
De son clair baiser de feu

Ainsi le chœur des romances
A la lèvre vole-t-il
Exclus-en si tu commences
Le réel parce que vil

Le sens trop précis rature
Ta vague littérature.

Who seeks, following the solitary leap
Till now external of our vagabond —
Verlaine? He's hidden in the grass, Verlaine

Only to find there in naive accord
With lip not drinking and with unchecked breath
A so shallow rivulet, much maligned death.

ALL THE SOUL INDRAWN . . .

All the soul indrawn
When slowly we exhale it
In many rounds of smoke
Lost in other rounds

Proves that some cigar
Burns skilfully how-so little
Its ash withdraws itself
From the clear kiss of fire

So the choir of songs
Flies it to your lip
Exclude if you begin
The real as being base

Its too sharp sense will overscrawl
Your vague literature.

AU SEUL SOUCI DE VOYAGER . . .

Au seul souci de voyager
Outre une Inde splendide et trouble
— Ce salut soit le messager
Du temps, cap que ta poupe double

Comme sur quelque vergue bas
Plongeante avec la caravelle
Écumait toujours en ébats
Un oiseau d'annonce nouvelle

Qui criait monotonement
Sans que la barre ne varie
Un inutile gisement
Nuit, désespoir et pierrerie

Par son chant reflété jusqu'au
Sourire du pâle Vasco.

TOUT ORGUEIL FUME-T-IL DU SOIR

Tout Orgueil fume-t-il du soir,
Torche dans un branle étouffée
Sans que l'immortelle bouffée
Ne puisse à l'abandon surseoir!

TO THE SOLE CARE OF VOYAGING . . .

To the sole care of voyaging
Beyond a splendid troubled Ind
— This greeting be the messenger
Of time, the cape your poop is doubling

As on some spar low down
Plunging with the caravel
There foamed ever in frolic
A bird of new tidings

Which cried monotonous
Though the helm veered not
A useless vein-lode
Night, despair, adamant

In its song reflected up to
The smile of pale Vasco.

DOES ALL PRIDE SMOKE OUT EVENING

Does all Pride smoke out evening,
A torch put out by a shake
Without the immortal jet
Surviving abandonment!

La chambre ancienne de l'hoir
De maint riche mais chu trophée
Ne serait pas même chauffée
S'il survenait par le couloir.

Affres du passé nécessaires
Agrippant comme avec des serres
Le sépulcre de désaveu,

Sous un marbre lourd qu'elle isole
Ne s'allume pas d'autre feu
Que la fulgurante console.

SURGI DE LA CROUPE ET DU BOND ...

Surgi de la croupe et du bond
D'une verrerie éphémère
Sans fleurir la veillée amère
Le col ignoré s'interrompt.

Je crois bien que deux bouches n'ont
Bu, ni son amant ni ma mère,
Jamais à la même Chimère,
Moi, sylphe de ce froid plafond!

Le pur vase d'aucun breuvage
Que l'inexhaustible veuvage
Agonise mais ne consent,

116

The ancient chamber of the heir
Of many a rich fall'n trophy
Would not even be warmed
If he came in by the passage.

Inevitable agonies of the past
Clutching as though with claws
Disavowal's sepulchre,

Under the heavy marble
It enisles no fire is lit
But the glittering console.

RISEN FROM THE SPRINGING CROUP . . .

Risen from the springing croup
Of a glass-work ephemeral
And the bitter vigil unflowered
The forgotten neck stops short.

I think that two mouths never,
Even her lover's and my mother's,
Drank from the same Chimaera,
I, sylph of this cold ceiling!

The pure vase of any potion
But the inexhaustible widowhood
Even in death consents not,

Naïf baiser des plus funèbres!
A rien expirer annonçant
Une rose dans les ténèbres.

UNE DENTELLE S'ABOLIT . . .

Une dentelle s'abolit
Dans le doute du Jeu suprême
A n'entr' ouvrir comme un blasphème
Qu'absence éternelle de lit.

Cet unanime blanc conflit
D'une guirlande avec la même,
Enfui contre la vitre blême
Flotte plus qu'il n'ensevelit.

Mais chez qui du rêve se dore
Tristement dort une mandore
Au creux néant musicien

Telle que vers quelque fenêtre
Selon nul ventre que le sien,
Filial on aurait pu naître.

Naive kiss funereal!
To breathe out anything announcing
A rose amid the darkness.

A LACE CURTAIN . . .

A lace curtain stands effaced
In doubt of the supreme Game
Unfolding like a blasphemy
On eternal bedlessness.

This unanimous white conflict
Of a garland with its like
Vanishing on the pallid glass
Is floating more than burying.

But with him where dreams are gilt
Sadly sleeps a mandola
Whose hollow void is musical

Such that towards some window pane
According to no womb but its,
Filial one might be born.

QUELLE SOIE AUX BAUMES DE TEMPS . . .

Quelle soie aux baumes de temps
Où la Chimère s'exténue
Vaut la torse et native nue
Que, hors de ton miroir, tu tends!

Les trous de drapeaux méditants
S'exaltent dans notre avenue:
Moi, j'ai ta chevelure nue
Pour enfouir mes yeux contents.

Non! La bouche ne sera sûre
De rien goûter à sa morsure,
S'il ne fait, ton princier amant,

Dans la considérable touffe
Expirer, comme un diamant,
Le cri des Gloires qu'il étouffe.

M'INTRODUIRE DANS TON HISTOIRE . . .

M'introduire dans ton histoire
C'est en héros effarouché
S'il a du talon nu touché
Quelque gazon de territoire

WHAT SILK EMBALMED BY TIME . . .

What silk embalmed by time
Whereon the Chimaera spreads
Equals the twisted native cloud
That, out of your mirror, you draw!

The holes of meditating flags
Are lifted in our avenue:
I, I have your naked hair
Wherein to plunge my eyes' content.

No! The mouth would not be sure
Of finding savour in its bite
Were he not, your princely lover,

In the considerable tuft
To breathe out, like a diamond,
The cry of Glories that he chokes.

TO GET MYSELF INTO YOUR STORY . . .

To get myself into your story
'Tis as a hero affrighted
Has his naked foot but touched
Some lawn of that territory

A des glaciers attentatoire
Je ne sais le naïf péché
Que tu n'auras pas empêché
De rire très haut sa victoire

Dis si je ne suis pas joyeux
Tonnerre et rubis aux moyeux
De voir en l'air que ce feu troue

Avec des royaumes épars
Comme mourir pourpre la roue
Du seul vespéral de mes chars

A LA NUE ACCABLANTE . . .

A la nue accablante tu
Basse de basalte et de laves
A même les échos esclaves
Par une trompe sans vertu

Quel sépulcral naufrage (tu
Le sais, écume, mais y baves)
Suprême une entre les épaves
Abolit le mât dévêtu

Ou cela que furibond faute
De quelque perdition haute
Tout l'abîme vain éployé

Violator of glaciers
I know no sin so naive be it
That you will not have prevented
From laughing's victory aloud

Say if I am not joyous
Thunder and rubies at the axles
To see in this fire-pierced air

Amid scattered realms
As though dying purple the wheel
Of my sole chariot of evening

TO THE OVERWHELMING BLACKNESS . . .

To the overwhelming blackness husht
Base of lava and basalt
Up to the echoes enslaved
By a virtueless trump

What sepulchral shipwreck (you
Know it, foam, but only slaver)
Supreme one among the flotsam
Abolished the disclad mast

Or that which furious (in default
Of some high perdition
With all the vain abyss let loose)

Dans le si blanc cheveu qui traîne
Avarement aura noyé
Le flanc enfant d'une sirène.

MES BOUQUINS REFERMÉS . . .

Mes bouquins refermés sur le nom de Paphos,
Il m'amuse d'élire avec le seul génie
Une ruine, par mille écumes bénie
Sous l'hyacinthe, au loin, de ses jours triomphaux.

Coure le froid avec ses silences de faux,
Je n'y hululerai pas de vide nénie
Si ce très blanc ébat au ras du sol dénie
A tout site l'honneur du paysage faux.

Ma faim qui d'aucuns fruits ici ne se régale
Trouve en leur docte manque une saveur égale:
Qu'un éclate de chair humain et parfumant!

Le pied sur quelque guivre où notre amour tisonne,
Je pense plus longtemps peut-être éperdument
A l'autre, au sein brûlé d'une antique amazone.

In the so white dragging hair
Will have drowned in niggard wise
Some young siren's infant flank.

MY OLD BOOKS CLOSED . . .

My old books closed on Paphos' name
By phantasy alone 'tis my whim to elect
A ruin, bless'd among a thousand foams
Under the hyacinth, far off, of its triumphant days.

Let the cold course with its scythe-like silences
I will not wail there for a vain reproach
Even if this so white gambol along the ground denies
To any site the honour of the unreal landscape.

My hunger, that on no fruit here regales
In their learn'd absence finds an equal taste:
Though one should burst with perfumed human flesh!

My foot on some *guivre* where our love warms its
    thoughts
I think for long, perhaps with ecstasy
Of the other, the seared breast of an antique amazon.

LE GUIGNON

Au-dessus du bétail ahuri des humains
Bondissaient en clartés les sauvages crinières
Des mendieurs d'azur le pied dans nos chemins.

Un noir vent sur leur marche éployé pour bannières
La flagellait de froid tel jusque dans la chair,
Qu'il y creusait aussi d'irritables ornières.

Toujours avec l'espoir de rencontrer la mer,
Ils voyageaient sans pain, sans bâtons et sans urnes,
Mordant au citron d'or de l'idéal amer.

La plupart râla dans les défilés nocturnes,
S'enivrant du bonheur de voir couler son sang,
O Mort le seul baiser aux bouches taciturnes!

Leur défaite, c'est par un ange très puissant
Debout à l'horizon dans le nu de son glaive:
Une pourpre se caille au sein reconnaissant.

Ils tettent la douleur comme ils tétaient le rêve
Et quand ils vont rythmant des pleurs voluptueux
Le peuple s'agenouille et leur mère se lève.

Ceux-là sont consolés, sûrs et majestueux;
Mais traînent à leurs pas cent frères qu'on bafoue,
Dérisoires martyrs de hasards tortueux.

Le sel pareil des pleurs ronge leur douce joue,
Ils mangent de la cendre avec le même amour,
Mais vulgaire ou bouffon le destin qui les roue.

Ils pouvaient exciter aussi comme un tambour
La servile pitié des races à voix ternes,
Égaux de Prométhée à qui manque un vautour!

Non, vils et fréquentant les déserts sans citerne,
Ils courent sous le fouet d'un monarque rageur,
Le Guignon, dont le rire inouï les prosterne.

Amants, il saute en croupe à trois, le partageur!
Puis le torrent franchi, vous plonge en une mare
Et laisse un bloc boueux du blanc couple nageur.

Grâce à lui, si l'un souffle à son buccin bizarre
Des enfants nous tordront en un rire obstiné
Qui, le poing à leur cul, singeront sa fanfare.

Grâce à lui, si l'une orne à point un sein fané
Par une rose qui nubile le rallume,
De la bave luira sur son bouquet damné.

Et ce squelette nain, coiffé d'un feutre à plume
Et botté, dont l'aisselle a pour poils vrais des vers,
Est pour eux l'infini de la vaste amertume.

Vexés ne vont-ils pas provoquer le pervers,
Leur rapière grinçant suit le rayon de lune
Qui neige en sa carcasse et qui passe au travers.

Désolés sans l'orgueil qui sacre l'infortune,
Et tristes de venger leurs os de coups de bec,
Ils convoitent la haine, au lieu de la rancune.

Ils sont l'amusement des racleurs de rebec,
Des marmots, des putains et de la vieille engeance
Des loqueteux dansant quand le broc est à sec.

Les poëtes bons pour l'aumône ou la vengeance,
Ne connaissant le mal de ces dieux effacés,
Les disent ennuyeux et sans intelligence.

'Ils peuvent fuir ayant de chaque exploit assez,
Comme un vierge cheval écume de tempête
Plutôt que de partir en galops cuirassés.

Nous soûlerons d'encens le vainqueur dans la fête:
Mais eux, pourquoi n'endosser pas, ces baladins,
D'écarlate haillon hurlant que l'on s'arrête!'

Quand en face tous leur ont craché les dédains,
Nuls et la barbe à mots bas priant le tonnerre,
Ces héros excédés de malaises badins

Vont ridiculement se pendre au réverbère.

PLACET FUTILE

Princesse! à jalouser le destin d'une Hébé
Qui poind sur cette tasse au baiser de vos lèvres,
J'use mes feux mais n'ai rang discret que d'abbé
Et ne figurerai même nu sur le Sèvres.

Comme je ne suis pas ton bichon embarbé,
Ni la pastille ni du rouge, ni jeux mièvres
Et que sur moi je sais ton regard clos tombé,
Blonde dont les coiffeurs divins sont des orfèvres!

Nommez-nous . . . toi de qui tant de ris framboisés
Se joignent en troupeau d'agneaux apprivoisés
Chez tous broutant les vœux et bêlant aux délires,

Nommez-nous . . . pour qu'Amour ailé d'un éventail
M'y peigne flûte aux doigts endormant ce bercail,
Princesse, nommez nous berger de vos sourires.

LE PITRE CHÂTIÉ

Yeux, lacs avec ma simple ivresse de renaître
Autre que l'histrion qui du geste évoquais
Comme plume la suie ignoble des quinquets,
J'ai troué dans le mur de toile une fenêtre.

De ma jambe et des bras limpide nageur traître,
A bonds multipliés, reniant le mauvais
Hamlet! c'est comme si dans l'onde j'innovais
Mille sépulcres pour y vierge disparaître.

Hilare or de cymbale à des poings irrité,
Tout à coup le soleil frappe la nudité
Qui pure s'exhala de ma fraîcheur de nacre,

Rance nuit de la peau quand sur moi vous passiez,
Ne sachant pas, ingrat! que c'était tout mon sacre,
Ce fard noyé dans l'eau perfide des glaciers.

UNE NÉGRESSE . . .

Une négresse par le démon secouée
Veut goûter une enfant triste de fruits nouveaux
Et criminels aussi sous leur robe trouée,
Cette goinfre s'apprête à de rusés travaux:

A son ventre compare heureuses deux tétines
Et, si haut que la main ne le saura saisir,
Elle darde le choc obscur de ses bottines
Ainsi que quelque langue inhabile au plaisir.

Contre la nudité peureuse de gazelle
Qui tremble, sur le dos tel un fol éléphant
Renversée elle attend et s'admire avec zèle,
En riant de ses dents naïves à l'enfant;

Et, dans ses jambes où la victime se couche,
Levant une peau noire ouverte sous le crin,
Avance le palais de cette étrange bouche
Pâle et rose comme un coquillage marin.

LES FENÊTRES

Las du triste hôpital, et de l'encens fétide
Qui monte en la blancheur banale des rideaux
Vers le grand crucifix ennuyé du mur vide,
Le moribond sournois y redresse un vieux dos,

Se traîne et va, moins pour chauffer sa pourriture
Que pour voir du soleil sur les pierres, coller
Les poils blancs et les os de la maigre figure
Aux fenêtres qu'un beau rayon clair veut hâler,

Et la bouche, fiévreuse et d'azur bleu vorace,
Telle, jeune, elle alla respirer son trésor,
Une peau virginale et de jadis! encrasse
D'un long baiser amer les tièdes carreaux d'or.

Ivre, il vit, oubliant l'horreur des saintes huiles,
Les tisanes, l'horloge et le lit infligé,
La toux; et quand le soir saigne parmi les tuiles,
Son œil, à l'horizon de lumière gorgé,

Voit des galères d'or, belles comme des cygnes,
Sur un fleuve de pourpre et de parfums dormir
En berçant l'éclair fauve et riche de leurs lignes
Dans un grand nonchaloir chargé de souvenir!

Ainsi, pris du dégoût de l'homme à l'âme dure
Vautré dans le bonheur, où ses seuls appétits
Mangent, et qui s'entête à chercher cette ordure
Pour l'offrir à la femme allaitant ses petits,

Je fuis et je m'accroche à toutes les croisées
D'où l'on tourne l'épaule à la vie, et, béni,
Dans leur verre, lavé d'éternelles rosées,
Que dore le matin chaste de l'Infini

Je me mire et me vois ange! et je meurs, et j'aime
— Que la vitre soit l'art, soit la mysticité —
A renaître, portant mon rêve en diadème,
Au ciel antérieur où fleurit la Beauté!

Mais, hélas! Ici-bas est maître: sa hantise
Vient m'écœurer parfois jusqu'en cet abri sûr,
Et le vomissement impur de la Bêtise
Me force à me boucher le nez devant l'azur.

Est-il moyen, ô Moi qui connais l'amertume,
D'enfoncer le cristal par le monstre insulté
Et de m'enfuir, avec mes deux ailes sans plume
— Au risque de tomber pendant l'éternité?

LES FLEURS

Des avalanches d'or du vieil azur, au jour
Premier et de la neige éternelle des astres
Jadis tu détachas les grands calices pour
La terre jeune encore et vierge de désastres,

Le glaïeul fauve, avec les cygnes au col fin,
Et ce divin laurier des âmes exilées
Vermeil comme le pur orteil du séraphin
Que rougit la pudeur des aurores foulées,

L'hyacinthe, le myrte à l'adorable éclair
Et, pareille à la chair de la femme, la rose
Cruelle, Hérodiade en fleur du jardin clair,
Celle qu'un sang farouche et radieux arrose!

Et tu fis la blancheur sanglotante des lys
Qui roulant sur des mers de soupirs qu'elle effleure
A travers l'encens bleu des horizons pâlis
Monte rêveusement vers la lune qui pleure!

Hosannah sur le cistre et dans les encensoirs,
Notre dame, hosannah du jardin de nos limbes!
Et finisse l'écho par les célestes soirs,
Extase des regards, scintillement des nimbes!

O Mère qui créas en ton sein juste et fort,
Calices balançant la future fiole,
De grandes fleurs avec la balsamique Mort
Pour le poëte las que la vie étiole.

RENOUVEAU

Le printemps maladif a chassé tristement
L'hiver, saison de l'art serein, l'hiver lucide,
Et dans mon être à qui le sang morne préside
L'impuissance s'étire en un long bâillement.

Des crépuscules blancs tiédissent sous mon crâne
Qu'un cercle de fer serre ainsi qu'un vieux tombeau
Et triste, j'erre après un rêve vague et beau,
Par les champs où la sève immense se pavane

Puis je tombe énervé de parfums d'arbres, las,
Et creusant de ma face une fosse à mon rêve,
Mordant la terre chaude où poussent les lilas,

J'attends, en m'abîmant que mon ennui s'élève . . .
— Cependant l'Azur rit sur la haie et l'éveil
De tant d'oiseaux en fleur gazouillant au soleil.

LE SONNEUR

Cependant que la cloche éveille sa voix claire
A l'air pur et limpide et profond du matin
Et passe sur l'enfant qui jette pour lui plaire
Un angelus parmi la lavande et le thym,

Le sonneur effleuré par l'oiseau qu'il éclaire,
Chevauchant tristement en geignant du latin
Sur la pierre qui tend la corde séculaire,
N'entend descendre à lui qu'un tintement lointain.

Je suis cet homme. Hélas! de la nuit désireuse,
J'ai beau tirer le câble à sonner l'Idéal,
De froids péchés s'ébat un plumage féal,

Et la voix ne me vient que par bribes et creuse!
Mais, un jour, fatigué d'avoir enfin tiré,
O Satan, j'ôterai la pierre et me pendrai.

TRISTESSE D'ÉTÉ

Le soleil, sur le sable, ô lutteuse endormie,
En l'or de tes cheveux chauffe un bain langoureux
Et, consumant l'encens sur ta joue ennemie,
Il mêle avec les pleurs un breuvage amoureux.

De ce blanc flamboiement l'immuable accalmie
T'a fait dire, attristée, ô mes baisers peureux,
'Nous ne serons jamais une seule momie
Sous l'antique désert et les palmiers heureux!'

Mais ta chevelure est une rivière tiède,
Où noyer sans frissons l'âme qui nous obsède
Et trouver ce Néant que tu ne connais pas!

Je goûterai le fard pleuré par tes paupières,
Pour voir s'il sait donner au cœur que tu frappas
L'insensibilité de l'azur et des pierres.

L'AZUR

De l'éternel azur la sereine ironie
Accable, belle indolemment comme les fleurs,
Le poëte impuissant qui maudit son génie
A travers un désert stérile de Douleurs.

Fuyant, les yeux fermés, je le sens qui regarde
Avec l'intensité d'un remords atterrant,
Mon âme vide. Où fuir? Et quelle nuit hagarde
Jeter, lambeaux, jeter sur ce mépris navrant?

Brouillards, montez! versez vos cendres monotones
Avec de longs haillons de brume dans les cieux
Qui noiera le marais livide des automnes
Et bâtissez un grand plafond silencieux!

Et toi, sors des étangs léthéens et ramasse
En t'en venant la vase et les pâles roseaux,
Cher Ennui, pour boucher d'une main jamais lasse
Les grands trous bleus que font méchamment les oiseaux.

Encor! que sans répit les tristes cheminées
Fument, et que de suie une errante prison
Éteigne dans l'horreur de ses noires traînées
Le soleil se mourant jaunâtre à l'horizon!

—Le Ciel est mort.—Vers toi, j'accours! donne,
    ô matière,
L'oubli de l'Idéal cruel et du Péché
A ce martyr qui vient partager la litière
Où le bétail heureux des hommes est couché,

Car j'y veux, puisque enfin ma cervelle, vidée
Comme le pot de fard gisant au pied d'un mur,
N'a plus l'art d'attifer la sanglotante idée,
Lugubrement bâiller vers un trépas obscur . . .

En vain! l'Azur triomphe, et je l'entends qui chante
Dans les cloches. Mon âme, il se fait voix pour plus
Nous faire peur avec sa victoire méchante,
Et du métal vivant sort en bleus angelus!

Il roule par la brume, ancien et traverse
Ta native agonie ainsi qu'un glaive sûr;
Où fuir dans la révolte inutile et perverse?
Je suis hanté. L'Azur! l'Azur! l'Azur! l'Azur!

AUMÔNE

Prends ce sac, Mendiant! tu ne le cajolas
Sénile nourrisson d'une tétine avare
Afin de pièce à pièce en égoutter ton glas.

Tire du métal cher quelque péché bizarre
Et vaste comme nous, les poings pleins, le baisons
Souffles-y qu'il se torde! une ardente fanfare.

Église avec l'encens que toutes ces maisons
Sur les murs quand berceur d'une bleue éclaircie
Le tabac sans parler roule les oraisons,

Et l'opium puissant brise la pharmacie!
Robes et peau, veux-tu lacérer le satin
Et boire en la salive heureuse l'inertie,

Par les cafés princiers attendre le matin?
Les plafonds enrichis de nymphes et de voiles,
On jette, au mendiant de la vitre, un festin.

Et quand tu sors, vieux dieu, grelottant sous tes toiles
D'emballage, l'aurore est un lac de vin d'or
Et tu jures avoir au gosier les étoiles!

Faute de supputer l'éclat de ton trésor,
Tu peux du moins t'orner d'une plume, à complies
Servir un cierge au saint en qui tu crois encor.

Ne t'imagine pas que je dis des folies.
La terre s'ouvre vieille à qui crève la faim.
Je hais une autre aumône et veux que tu m'oublies

Et surtout ne va pas, frère, acheter du pain.

139

PROSE

pour des Esseintes

Hyperbole! de ma mémoire
Triomphalement ne sais-tu
Te lever, aujourd'hui grimoire
Dans un livre de fer vêtu:

Car j'installe, par la science,
L'hymne des cœurs spirituels
En l'œuvre de ma patience,
Atlas, herbiers et rituels.

Nous promenions notre visage
(Nous fûmes deux, je le maintiens)
Sur maints charmes de paysage,
O sœur, y comparant les tiens.

L'ère d'autorité se trouble
Lorsque, sans nul motif, on dit
De ce midi que notre double
Inconscience approfondit

Que, sol des cent iris, son site,
Ils savent s'il a bien été,
Ne porte pas de nom que cite
L'or de la trompette d'Été.

Oui, dans une île que l'air charge
De vue et non de visions
Toute fleur s'étalait plus large
Sans que nous en devisions.

Telles, immenses, que chacune
Ordinairement se para
D'un lucide contour, lacune
Qui des jardins la sépara.

Gloire du long désir, Idées
Tout en moi s'exaltait de voir
La famille des iridées
Surgir à ce nouveau devoir,

Mais cette sœur sensée et tendre
Ne porta son regard plus loin
Que sourire et, comme à l'entendre
J'occupe mon antique soin.

Oh! sache l'Esprit de litige,
A cette heure où nous nous taisons,
Que de lis multiples la tige
Grandissait trop pour nos raisons

Et non comme pleure la rive,
Quand son jeu monotone ment
A vouloir que l'ampleur arrive
Parmi mon jeune étonnement

D'ouïr tout le ciel et la carte
Sans fin attestés sur mes pas,
Par le flot même qui s'écarte,
Que ce pays n'exista pas.

L'enfant abdique son extase
Et docte déjà par chemins
Elle dit le mot: Anastase!
Né pour d'éternels parchemins,

Avant qu'un sépulcre ne rie
Sous aucun climat, son aïeul,
De porter ce nom: Pulchérie!
Caché par le trop grand glaïeul.

ÉVENTAIL

de Madame Mallarmé

Avec comme pour langage
Rien qu'un battement aux cieux
Le futur vers se dégage
Du logis très précieux

Aile tout bas la courrière
Cet éventail si c'est lui
Le même par qui derrière
Toi quelque miroir a lui

Limpide (où va redescendre
Pourchassée en chaque grain
Un peu d'invisible cendre
Seule à me rendre chagrin)

Toujours tel il apparaisse
Entre tes mains sans paresse.

FEUILLET D'ALBUM

Tout à coup et comme par jeu
Mademoiselle qui voulûtes
Ouïr se révéler un peu
Le bois de mes diverses flûtes

Il me semble que cet essai
Tenté devant un paysage
A du bon quand je le cessai
Pour vous regarder au visage

Oui ce vain souffle que j'exclus
Jusqu'à la dernière limite
Selon mes quelques doigts perclus
Manque de moyens s'il imite

Votre très naturel et clair
Rire d'enfant qui charme l'air.

SONNET

Dame
      sans trop d'ardeur à la fois enflammant
La rose qui cruelle ou déchirée et lasse
Même du blanc habit de pourpre le délace
Pour ouïr dans sa chair pleurer le diamant

Oui sans ces crises de rosée et gentiment
Ni brise quoique, avec, le ciel orageux passe
Jalouse d'apporter je ne sais quel espace
Au simple jour le jour très vrai du sentiment.

Ne te semble-t-il pas, disons, que chaque année
Dont sur ton front renaît la grâce spontanée
Suffise selon quelque apparence et pour moi

Comme un éventail frais dans la chambre s'étonne
A raviver du peu qu'il faut ici d'émoi
Toute notre native amitié monotone.

SONNET

O si chère de loin et proche et blanche, si
Délicieusement toi, Mary, que je songe
A quelque baume rare émané par mensonge
Sur aucun bouquetier de cristal obscurci

Le sais-tu, oui! pour moi voici des ans, voici
Toujours que ton sourire éblouissant prolonge
La même rose avec son bel été qui plonge
Dans autrefois et puis dans le futur aussi.

Mon cœur qui dans les nuits parfois cherche à s'entendre
Ou de quel dernier mot t'appeler le plus tendre
S'exalte en celui rien que chuchoté de sœur

N'était, très grand trésor et tête si petite,
Que tu m'enseignes bien toute une autre douceur
Tout bas par le baiser seul dans tes cheveux dite.

REMÉMORATION D'AMIS BELGES

A des heures et sans que tel souffle l'émeuve
Toute la vétusté presque couleur encens
Comme furtive d'elle et visible je sens
Que se dévêt pli selon pli la pierre veuve

Flotte ou semble par soi n'apporter une preuve
Sinon d'épandre pour baume antique le temps
Nous immémoriaux quelques-uns si contents
Sur la soudaineté de notre amitié neuve

O très chers rencontrés en le jamais banal
Bruges multipliant l'aube au défunt canal
Avec la promenade éparse de maint cygne

Quand solennellement cette cité m'apprit
Lesquels entre ses fils un autre vol désigne
A prompte irradier ainsi qu'aile l'esprit.

CHANSONS BAS

I
LE SAVETIER

Hors de la poix rien à faire,
Le lys naît blanc, comme odeur
Simplement je le préfère
A ce bon raccommodeur.

Il va de cuir à ma paire
Adjoindre plus que je n'eus
Jamais, cela désespère
Un besoin de talons nus.

Son marteau qui ne dévie
Fixe de clous gouailleurs
Sur la semelle l'envie
Toujours conduisant ailleurs.

Il recréerait des souliers,
O pieds! si vous le vouliez.

II

LA MARCHANDE D'HERBES AROMATIQUES
Ta paille azur de lavandes,
Ne crois pas avec ce cil
Osé que tu me la vendes
Comme à l'hypocrite s'il

En tapisse la muraille
De lieux les absolus lieux
Pour le ventre qui se raille
Renaître aux sentiments bleus.

Mieux entre une envahissante
Chevelure ici mets-la
Que le brin salubre y sente,
Zéphirine, Paméla

Ou conduise vers l'époux
Les prémices de tes poux.

III
LE CANTONNIER
Ces cailloux, tu les nivelles
Et c'est, comme troubadour,
Un cube aussi de cervelles
Qu'il me faut ouvrir par jour.

IV
LE MARCHAND D'AIL ET D'OIGNONS
L'ennui d'aller en visite
Avec l'ail nous l'éloignons.
L'élégie au pleur hésite
Peu si je fends des oignons.

V
LA FEMME DE L'OUVRIER
La femme, l'enfant, la soupe
En chemin pour le carrier
Le complimentent qu'il coupe
Dans l'us de se marier.

VI
LE VITRIER
Le pur soleil qui remise
Trop d'éclat pour l'y trier
Ote ébloui sa chemise
Sur le dos du vitrier.

VII
LE CRIEUR D'IMPRIMÉS
Toujours, n'importe le titre,
Sans même s'enrhumer au
Dégel, ce gai siffle-litre
Crie un premier numéro.

VIII
LA MARCHANDE D'HABITS
Le vif œil dont tu regardes
Jusques à leur contenu
Me sépare de mes hardes
Et comme un dieu je vais **nu**.

BILLET A WHISTLER

Pas les rafales à propos
De rien comme occuper la rue
Sujette au noir vol de chapeaux;
Mais une danseuse apparue

Tourbillon de mousseline ou
Fureur éparses en écumes
Que soulève par son genou
Celle même dont nous vécûmes

Pour tout, hormis lui, rebattu
Spirituelle, ivre, immobile
Foudroyer avec le tutu,
Sans se faire autrement de bile

Sinon rieur que puisse l'air
De sa jupe éventer Whistler.

RONDELS

I

Rien au réveil que vous n'ayez
Envisagé de quelque moue
Pire si le rire secoue
Votre aile sur les oreillers

Indifféremment sommeillez
Sans crainte qu'une haleine avoue
Rien au réveil que vous n'ayez
Envisagé de quelque moue

Tous les rêves émerveillés
Quand cette beauté les déjoue
Ne produisent fleur sur la joue
Dans l'œil diamants impayés
Rien au réveil que vous n'ayez

Si tu veux nous nous aimerons
Avec tes lèvres sans le dire
Cette rose ne l'interromps
Qu'à verser un silence pire

Jamais de chants ne lancent prompts
Le scintillement du sourire
Si tu veux nous nous aimerons
Avec tes lèvres sans le dire

Muet muet entre les ronds
Sylphe dans la pourpre d'empire
Un baiser flambant se déchire
Jusqu'aux pointes des ailerons
Si tu veux nous nous aimerons

PETIT AIR II

Indomptablement a dû
Comme mon espoir s'y lance
Eclater là-haut perdu
Avec furie et silence,

Voix étrangère au bosquet
Ou par nul écho suivie,

L'oiseau qu'on n'ouït jamais
Une autre fois en la vie.

Le hagard musicien,
Cela dans le doute expire
Si de mon sein pas du sien
A jailli le sanglot pire

Déchiré va-t-il entier
Rester sur quelque sentier!

PETIT AIR (GUERRIER)

Ce me va hormis l'y taire
Que je sente du foyer
Un pantalon militaire
A ma jambe rougeoyer

L'invasion je la guette
Avec le vierge courroux
Tout juste de la baguette
Au gant blanc des tourlourous

Nue ou d'écorce tenace
Pas pour battre le Teuton
Mais comme une autre menace
A la fin que me veut-on

De trancher ras cette ortie
Folle de la sympathie.

HOMMAGE

Le silence déjà funèbre d'une moire
Dispose plus qu'un pli seul sur le mobilier
Que doit un tassement du principal pilier
Précipiter avec le manque de mémoire.

Notre si vieil ébat triomphal du grimoire,
Hiéroglyphes dont s'exalte le millier
A propager de l'aile un frisson familier!
Enfouissez-le-moi plutôt dans une armoire.

Du souriant fracas originel haï
Entre elles de clartés maîtresses a jailli
Jusque vers un parvis né pour leur simulacre,

Trompettes tout haut d'or pâmé sur les vélins,
Le dieu Richard Wagner irradiant un sacre
Mal tu par l'encre même en sanglots sibyllins.

HOMMAGE

Toute Aurore même gourde
A crisper un poing obscur
Contre des clairons d'azur
Embouchés par cette sourde

A le pâtre avec la gourde
Jointe au bâton frappant dur
Le long de son pas futur
Tant que la source ample sourde

Par avance ainsi tu vis
O solitaire Puvis
De Chavannes
                    jamais seul

De conduire le temps boire
A la nymphe sans linceul
Que lui découvre ta Gloire.

ÉVENTAIL

De frigides roses pour vivre
Toutes la même interrompront
Avec un blanc calice prompt
Votre souffle devenu givre

Mais que mon battement délivre
La touffe par un choc profond
Cette frigidité se fond
En du rire de fleurir ivre

A jeter le ciel en détail
Voilà comme bon éventail
Tu conviens mieux qu'une fiole

Nul n'enfermant à l'émeri
Sans qu'il y perde ou le viole
L'arôme émané de Méry.

UN COUP DE DÉS
JAMAIS N'ABOLIRA
LE HASARD

PRÉFACE

J'AIMERAIS qu'on ne lût pas cette Note ou que parcourue, même on l'oubliât; elle apprend, au Lecteur habile, peu de chose situé outre sa pénétration: mais, peut troubler l'ingénu devant appliquer un regard aux premiers mots du Poëme pour que de suivants, disposés comme ils sont, l'amènent aux derniers, le tout sans nouveauté qu'un espacement de la lecture. Les 'blancs' en effet, assument l'importance, frappent d'abord; la versification en exigea, comme silence alentour, ordinairement, au point qu'un morceau, lyrique ou de peu de pieds, occupe, au milieu, le tiers environ du feuillet: je ne transgresse cette mesure, seulement la disperse. Le papier intervient chaque fois qu'une image d'elle-même cesse ou rentre, acceptant la succession d'autres et, comme il ne s'agit pas, ainsi que toujours, de traits sonores réguliers ou vers — plutôt, de subdivisions prismatiques de l'Idée, l'instant de paraître et que dure leur concours, dans quelque mise en scène spirituelle exacte, c'est à des places variables, près ou loin du fil conducteur latent, en raison de la vraisemblance, que s'impose le texte.

L'avantage, si j'ai droit à le dire, littéraire, de cette distance copiée qui mentalement sépare des groupes de
mots ou les mots entre eux, semble d'accélérer tantôt
et de ralentir le mouvement, le scandant, l'intimant
même selon une vision simultanée de la Page: celle-ci
prise pour unité comme l'est autre part le Vers ou ligne
parfaite. La fiction affleurera et se dissipera, vite, d'après
la mobilité de l'écrit, autour des arrêts fragmentaires
d'une phrase capitale dès le titre introduite et continuée.
Tout se passe, par raccourci, en hypothèse; on évite le
récit. Ajouter que de cet emploi à nu de la pensée avec
retraits, prolongements, fuites, ou son dessin même,
résulte, pour qui veut lire à haute voix, une partition.
La différence des caractères d'imprimerie entre le motif
prépondérant, un secondaire et d'adjacents, dicte son
importance à l'émission orale et la portée, moyenne, en
haut, en bas de page, notera que monte ou descend
l'intonation. Seules certaines directions très hardies, des
empiètements, etc., formant le contre-point de cette
prosodie, demeurent dans une œuvre, qui manque de
précédents, à l'état élémentaire: non que j'estime l'op-
portunité d'essais timides; mais il ne m'appartient pas,
hormis une pagination spéciale ou de volume à moi,
dans un Périodique, même valeureux, gracieux et invitant qu'il se montre aux belles libertés, d'agir par trop
contrairement à l'usage. J'aurai, toutefois, indiqué du
Poëme ci-joint, mieux que l'esquisse, un 'état' qui ne
rompe pas de tous points avec la tradition; poussé sa

présentation en maint sens aussi avant qu'elle n'offusque personne: suffisamment, pour ouvrir des yeux. Aujourd'hui ou sans présumer de l'avenir qui sortira d'ici, rien ou presque un art, reconnaissons aisément que la tentative participe, avec imprévu, de poursuites particulières et chères à notre temps, le vers libre et le poëme en prose. Leur réunion s'accomplit sous une influence, je sais, étrangère, celle de la Musique entendue au concert; on en retrouve plusieurs moyens m'ayant semblé appartenir aux Lettres, je les reprends. Le genre, que c'en devienne un comme la symphonie, peu à peu, à côté du chant personnel, laisse intact l'antique vers, auquel je garde un culte et attribue l'empire de la passion et des rêveries; tandis que ce serait le cas de traiter, de préférence (ainsi qu'il suit) tels sujets d'imagination pure et complexe ou intellect: que ne reste aucune raison d'exclure de la Poésie — unique source.

UN COUP DE DÉS

JAMAIS

QUAND BIEN MÊME LANCÉ DANS DES

CIRCONSTANCES ÉTERNELLES

DU FOND D'UN NAUFRAGE

161

SOIT
    que

               l'Abîme

   blanchi
        étale
          furieux

                    sous une inclinaison
                      plane désespérément

                              d'aile

                          la sienne
                              par

avance retombée d'un mal à dresser le vol
  et couvrant les jaillissements
      coupant au ras les bonds

  très à l'intérieur résume

                    [alternative
l'ombre enfouie dans la profondeur par cette voile

            jusqu'adapter
              à l'envergure

  sa béante profondeur en tant que la coque

    d'un bâtiment

    penché de l'un ou l'autre bord

163

LE MAÎTRE

surgi
    inférant

          de cette conflagration

            que se

          comme on menace

l'unique Nombre qui ne peut pas

                hésite
          cadavre par le bras
plutôt
    que de jouer
        en maniaque chenue
          la partie
        au nom des flots

                un

        naufrage cela

hors d'anciens calculs
où la manœuvre avec l'âge oubliée

jadis il empoignait la barre

à ses pieds
de l'horizon unanime
prépare
s'agite et mêle
au poing qui l'étreindrait
un destin et les vents

être un autre
Esprit
pour le jeter
dans la tempête
en reployer la division et passer fier

écarté du secret qu'il détient

envahit le chef
coule en barbe soumise
direct de l'homme
sans nef
n'importe
où vaine

165

ancestralement à n'ouvrir pas la main
                                    crispée
                        par delà l'inutile tête
              legs en la disparition
                          à quelqu'un
                                        ambigu
                    l'ultérieur démon immémorial
ayant
        de contrées nulles
                          induit
                                        [probabilité
le vieillard vers cette conjonction suprême avec la
                          celui
                          son ombre puérile
caressée et polie et rendue et lavée
                          assouplie par la vague et soustraite
                          aux durs os perdus entre les ais
                          né
                                    d'un ébat
la mer par l'aïeul tentant ou l'aïeul contre la mer
                    une chance oiseuse
                                        Fiançailles
dont
        le voile d'illusion rejailli leur hantise
        ainsi que le fantôme d'un geste
                              chancellera
                              s'affalera
                                        folie

N'ABOLIRA

COMME SI

Une insinuation

au silence

dans quelque proche

voltige

simple

enroulée avec ironie
                ou
                        le mystère
                                        précipité
                                                hurlé

tourbillon d'hilarité et d'horreur

autour du gouffre
                        sans le joncher
                                        ni fuir

                et en berce le vierge indice

                                COMME SI

plume solitaire éperdue

sauf

que la rencontre ou l'effleure une toque de minuit
et immobilise
au velours chiffonné par un esclaffement sombre

cette blancheur rigide

dérisoire

en opposition au ciel
trop
pour ne pas marquer
exigüment
quiconque

prince amer de l'écueil

s'en coiffe comme de l'héroïque
irrésistible mais contenu
par sa petite raison virile
en foudre

soucieux

      expiatoire et pubère

                  muet

              La lucide et seigneuriale aigrette
                    au front invisible
        scintille
              puis ombrage
     une stature mignonne ténébreuse
       en sa torsion de sirène

     par d'impatientes squames ultimes

rire

que

SI

de vertige

debout

le temps
de souffleter
bifurquées

un roc

faux manoir
tout de suite
évaporé en brumes

qui imposa
une borne à l'infini

173

C'ÉTAIT
issu stellaire

CE SERAIT
    pire
        non
            davantage ni moins
                indifféremment mais autant

LE NOMBRE

EXISTÂT-IL
autrement qu'hallucination éparse d'agonie

COMMENÇÂT-IL ET CESSÂT-IL
sourdant que nié et clos quand apparu
enfin
par quelque profusion répandue en rareté
SE CHIFFRÂT-IL

évidence de la somme pour peu qu'une
ILLUMINÂT-IL

LE HASARD

Choit
la plume
rythmique suspens du sinistre
s'ensevelir
aux écumes originelles
naguères d'où sursauta son délire jusqu'à une cime
flétrie
par la neutralité identique du gouffre

175

RIEN

de la mémorable crise
ou se fût
l'événement

accompli en vue de tout résultat nul

humain

N'AURA EU LIEU
une élévation ordinaire verse l'absence

QUE LE LIEU

inférieur clapotis quelconque comme pour disperser
l'acte vide]   abruptement qui sinon
par son mensonge
eût fondé
la perdition

dans ces parages
du vague
en quoi toute réalité se dissout

EXCEPTÉ

    à l'altitude

        PEUT-ÊTRE

           aussi loin qu'un endroit

fusionne avec au delà

                    hors l'intérêt

               quant à lui signalé

                           en général

selon telle obliquité par telle déclivité

                           de feux

       vers

          ce doit être

            le Septentrion aussi Nord

                  UNE CONSTELLATION

          froide d'oubli et de désuétude

                    pas tant

                 qu'elle n'énumère

      sur quelque surface vacante et supérieure

             le heurt successif

                    sidéralement

       d'un compte total en formation

veillant

       doutant

           roulant

              brillant et méditant

                   avant de s'arrêter

          à quelque point dernier qui le sacre

          Toute Pensée émet un Coup de Dés

COMMENTARIES ON THE POEMS
BY CHARLES MAURON

SALUTATION

In his Bibliography of 1898 [1] Mallarmé writes: '*Salutation*—This Sonnet, in proposing a toast, recently, at a
dinner of *La Plume* (a paper) at which I had the honour
to preside.'

The poem is therefore a toast, without more importance or weight in the poet's mind than the foam of the
champagne in his raised glass. 'Nothing! this foam . . .'
and as its whiteness outlines the cup, so too the verse
only 'designates' it.

But at once the word 'foam' evokes resonances of the
sea. Mallarmé sees in this bubbly foam a troop of sirens
plunging and splashing. He liked the humorous sensuality of such evocations, as for instance in the *Faune*:

> 'This flight of swans, no, Naiads, fled
> Or plunged . . .'

It is the same evocation of the whiteness of bodies
and the same amused smile; only here the word 'siren,'
implying the sea, allows him to glide to the following
idea. A sea voyage is an adventure; and an adventure too

[1] Inserted by Mallarmé himself at the end of his volume of
collected poems, published in that year.

is the literary life of a group of young men — Argonauts setting out to grasp the Golden Fleece. This gives us the essential metaphor of the poem. Mallarmé develops it with easy mastery, with that half-lyrical, half-humorous genius which is his peculiar gift. The word 'rolling' (*tangage*) connected with drunkenness underlines the fact that he is still really talking about the wine.

In the French text, the syntax is condensed, as always, but offers no serious difficulty. The end of the poem may be set out prosaically thus:

> 'De porter debout ce salut à ce qui valut — solitude, récif, étoile, n'importe! — le blanc souci de notre toile.'

LE PITRE CHÂTIÉ

Most of the obscurities in this poem are made clear by a first version which was published by Dr. Bonniot, the son-in-law of Mallarmé, in the *Revue de France* of April 15th 1929. It runs as follows:

> 'Pour ses yeux, — pour nager dans ces lacs, dont les quais
> Sont plantés de beaux cils qu'un matin bleu pénètre,
> J'ai, Muse, moi, ton pitre, — enjambé la fenêtre
> Et fui notre baraque où fument tes quinquets.
>
> Et d'herbes enivré, j'ai plongé comme un traître
> Dans ces lacs défendus, et, quand tu m'appelais,

Baigné mes membres nus dans l'onde aux blancs galets,
Oubliant mon habit de pitre au tronc d'un hêtre.

Le soleil du matin séchait mon corps nouveau
Et je sentais fraîchir loin de ta tyrannie
La neige des glaciers dans ma chair assainie,

Ne sachant pas, hélas! quand s'en allait sur l'eau
Le suif de mes cheveux et le fard de ma peau,
Muse, que cette crasse était tout le génie!'

The general idea is thus made plain: the eyes of the
beloved are compared with a pure water in which the
poet hopes to wash away the effects of his literary barn-
storming — but the thing has its dangers, for it is difficult to distinguish between the player and the artist,
the disguise and the genius.

Here are some isolated difficulties:

1st *Quatrain*. 'Autre que l'histrion qui du geste évoquais — Comme plume la suie ignoble des quinquets':
different from the mountebank that I was, whose gestures revealed — as clearly as though it had been written
large — the booth in which I play before the smoking
footlights.

2nd *Quatrain*. '. . . c'est comme si dans l'onde j'innovais — Mille sépulcres . . .' with each stroke the
swimmer seems to carve a new grave in the water; he

plunges in, is purified, and leaves behind the dead self of the bad actor whom he flies.

1st Tercet. With a great burst of laughter, like a clashing of cymbals shaken together at the wrists, the sun strikes me as I leave the freshness of the water.

2nd Tercet. 'Rance nuit de la peau quand sur moi vous passiez — Ne sachant pas, ingrat! que c'était tout mon sacre' means: For I, ungrateful that I am, did not know that in letting my skin be darkened with rancid greasepaint I was in fact duly annointed.

SIGH

(These appear to be Roger Fry's original notes. Such notes exist on a few of the other poems, but have been superseded by M. Mauron's commentaries.)

Line 2. The literal translation is, of course, 'an autumn, splashed with freckles,' but 'taches de rousseur' conveys a colour sensation which is lacking in 'freckles' and 'russet' is necessary to complete the image.

Line 5. 'L'Azur.' Even here this has a certain symbolic character which is not adequately rendered by 'the blue.' Metrical necessities have here interfered with exact translation.

Line 6. 'Attendri' used of the sky seems to have no exact correspondence in English. 'Pitiful' or 'gentle' conveys the general sense but is too particularised.

SONNET (— 'Sur les bois oubliés . . .')

Commentary is scarcely needed on this sonnet. It is the dead woman who speaks, as the quotation marks indicate. She addresses the survivor, 'lonely threshold's prisoner,' since the fact of his being alive forbids his passing the threshold of the sepulchre to take his place there.

In the verse 'alone with the lack of great posies is loaded' there sounds, for the first time in this selection, the peculiarly Mallarméan note, with its sadness and purity. Hitherto the sensitive ear will have felt echoes of Baudelaire even in the *Brise Marine*, where the taste for exotic nature and the desire to set sail, even towards disaster, seems borrowed from the poet of *Les Fleurs du Mal*:

'O Mort, vieux capitaine, il est temps! levons l'ancre!
Ce pays nous ennuie, ô Mort! Appareillons!' [2]

But Baudelaire would never have written 'loaded with the lack of great posies.' This method of condensing, in words of negation, not only the familiar idea, 'It's impossible in winter to find flowers for our dead,' but also the intense desire to find them all the same, of the man who peoples this void with imaginary blossoms, and loads the bare stone with their ideal abundance: this

[2] Baudelaire, *Fleurs du Mal*, 'Le Voyage':
'Oh Death, old captain, it is time we weighed anchor!
We are weary of this country, oh Death! Let us sail!'

method, I say, belongs only to Mallarmé. French poetry had hitherto heard nothing like it. Moreover the whole atmosphere of the sonnet seems to me significant: this bourgeois room where some one at midnight, his eyes fixed on the dying embers, murmurs, for himself alone, a secret name, a magic expression of his most intimate feeling, is a situation such as the reader will find throughout Mallarmé even in the most abstract of the *Divagations:*

'Méditatif:
Il est (tisonne-t-on) un art . . .' (*Crayonné au théâtre*.) [8]

GIFT OF A POEM

All night Mallarmé has been working at a poem, which is none other than the *Herodias,* since it spoke of Idumea ('child of an Idumaean night'). And all night long he has seen his window 'burnt with aromatics and gold' — the reflection of his lamp and the effect of the oriental atmosphere.[4] But the pane grows pale. The dawn breaks in. At first it is like a wounded bird 'black, with wing bleeding, pale and unfeathered.' Then the

[8] 'Meditative:
There is (one fire-stirs) an art . . .'(*Pencilled at the theatre.*)

[4]   . . . my hairs, which are not flowers,
To spread forgetfulness of human ills,
But gold, for ever virgin of *aromatics* . . . (HERODIAS.)

lamp fades to a pale angelic vision under the outbursts of triumphant light — 'Palms!' [5]

Then the poet can see his work, the poem which has just been born. He finds it horrible (like many new-born things) although he tries to smile on it. What is he to do with it? Mme. Mallarmé is asleep in the next room. She also clasps to her breast her infant daughter. And the symmetry of this situation excites the poet's emotion tinged with humour. 'Here then is my new child, borne by me. Will you accept and adopt it and speak to it with your mother's musical voice? Will you give it suck? It comes from the "virgin azure" and this morning air makes it hungry.'

HERODIAS: SCENE

I have insisted adequately in the Introduction on the deeper significance of *Herodias* not to need to dwell any further on it here. The object of these commentaries, let me repeat, is not a study of these poems but an explanation of their difficulties. The language of *Herodias* is sufficiently clear without comment. A few notes will be enough.

The sense of the first verse:

'Alive! or is it the shadow of a princess I see?'

---

[5] An interjection in apposition to dawn.

is given by what follows: Herodias has gone into the
lion's cage —

'Down into the heavy prison of iron and stone' —

and the nurse had not hoped to see her return.[6]

Perhaps the reader will follow the poem more easily
if he knows that it is constructed according to a rigid
plan. First, three gestures, or rather three attempts at
gestures, on the part of the nurse, arouse in Herodias a
growing fear and anger. The old woman tries to kiss
her hand, to perfume her hair, and to touch her tresses,
a triple 'impiety' in which the princess, who has reacted
against each of the gestures, sees a sinister omen:

'This kiss, these offered scents, and, shall I say it?
My heart, this hand still more sacrilegious,
For I think you would have touched me, make a day
That will not finish without ill on the tower.'

Second, poetically, the gestures of the nurse appear
as premonitions of a graver menace, that of a lover's
embrace:

'I should love
To be for whom Destiny guards your secrets.'

The old woman foresees this and tries to prepare
Herodias, first by irony and then by pity. She only provokes a fierce revolt:

[6] Probably Mallarmé had in mind the legend that lions will not
harm a virgin.

'No, it's for me, for me that I flower, deserted!'

a passage that is the centre of the poem.

Third, after the preparation of a more intimate scene — the curtains drawn and the candles lighted — the nurse goes. Herodias, alone, admits to herself:

> 'You lie, naked flower
> Of my lips.'

This finishes this first part (of what seems to have been intended as a much longer work).

Let me add that to my mind there has been too much insistence on the Parnassian character of this poem, in which M. Thibaudet sees principally a 'competition piece.' The jewels of the Parnassians are well-cut, sparkling stones, but without the shifting lights of Mallarmé's poem. Leconte de Lisle, Hérédia, Gautier seem as far as it is possible to be from any expression of secret psychological phenomena. They cut their verses like skilled craftsmen, without great violence and without clumsiness. *Herodias*, on the other hand, in spite of its verbal splendours, seems to me one of the most bizarre, gauche, and, if one can use the word, the most 'submarine' poems in the French language. One cannot understand it at all completely unless one realises that the poet is in communication with some unconscious depths. No Parnassian hero would ever have sought in a mirror 'memories like leaves.' Never, above all, under the pressure of unconscious impulses, would a Parnassian have invented so unlifelike a dialogue. For the unreality is here a proof of sincerity. Let me say that for my part I find in *Herodias* the effect of a dream. A psychoanalyst would explain the poem better than a literary critic. I believe, to be more precise, that the nurse symbolises, vaguely, the natural life and its temptations; not directly, but, as in Freudian theory, by an evocation of early childhood. For the Mallarmé of *Herodias* the earthly paradise is in the past, and towards that lost Eden the princess, in spite of herself, turns her eyes:

> 'But who would touch me, of the lions untouched?
> Besides, I want naught human, and if sculptured
> You see me with eyes lost in Paradise
> 'Tis when I bring to mind your milk once drunk.'

Almost all the familiar ideas of modern psychology find, for that matter, some example in the symbols of this poem. After the repression of unconscious desires, after the return to childhood,[7] how can we avoid thinking of narcissism in reading the famous invocation to the mirror. How can we avoid remembering the moon cult of Salambô and the ambivalence of the serpent (at once icy cold and phallic) before the 'inviolate reptile' of Herodias, or her invocation of the cold star [the moon]:

[7] See Introduction, page 20 et seq.

'And your lonely sister, oh my sister eternal
My dream will mount you-ward.'

I cannot attempt even to sketch a study of this kind, for which I lack all knowledge.[8] But if esthetic one day becomes a branch of psychology — and, after all, this is the only way in which we shall avoid mere gossip, since all that is not an art should become a science — I cannot help believing that *Herodias* will provide one of the clearest examples for the new criticism.

CANTICLE OF ST. JOHN

This poem forms part of *Herodias*, of which we possess only two fragments. It treats, therefore, of St. John the Baptist. The essential idea of the poem was evidently suggested to Mallarmé by the fact that St. John's Day coincides well enough with the summer solstice. It consists then of a single metaphor which compares on the one hand the sun's trajectory, first ascending and then descending after an imperceptible halt, a hesitation at the culminating point and moment of supreme exaltation (implied in the word solstice) — and, on the other hand, the trajectory traced by the head of St. John at the moment of decollation.

[8] PUBLISHER'S NOTE: This was written in 1936. M. Mauron has since devoted much further study to Mallarmé, and has published a book, *Introduction à la Psychanalyse de Mallarmé* (Neuchatel-Paris, 1950; La Baconnière).

The first stanza, with admirable brevity, sets forth the theme of ascension and descent (the latter rendered more abrupt by the rhythm). This gives the first, the sun-term of the metaphor. The second stanza expresses the sensations of decollation. With the third stanza the head begins its solitary wide-eyed ('vigie') ascent; the strange use of the word 'scythe' in place of the more appropriate word 'sword' is to be explained first as the symbol of Death; secondly, this blade, shaped like a long-pointed wing, permits the expression 'triumphant flights' which poetically reinforces the uprush of the head. But the head is the seat of the spirit and soul; thus decollation and ascension prolong and consecrate, by this 'rupture clean,' the Saint's ancient struggle between flesh and spirit. Asceticism, fasting, and the ascent towards the light and frozen purity ('surpassing that of glaciers') complete each other reciprocally and find their symbol in the leap of the head towards the heights. These ideas inform the movement of the third, fourth and fifth stanzas. Now the culminating point is reached: as the sun descends again, the head falls. In this fall it bows and appears to bend so as to receive baptism. And such indeed it receives, and by its inclination salutes the first principle, God and sun — which christens it with its rays. As in the first stanza, where the theme is given, and in conformity with the constantly repeated rhythm, the movement of the end is much more abrupt than that of the ascent. So strict a correspondence, so severe an architectural design give to this short piece a plenitude which astonishes one at each fresh reading. Irresistibly one thinks of J. S. Bach.

Note. — If the poem were punctuated there would be a full stop after the fourth stanza. At the beginning of the fifth, in the French 'Qu'elle' marks an exclamation; 'elle' ('it') refers back to 'tête' ('head') of the third stanza.

THE AFTERNOON OF A FAUN

A faun lies asleep under the thick boughs of a wood in Sicily. Around him the landscape is burnt by the fierce light of a summer afternoon. The Faun half wakes. He has been dreaming of the rape of nymphs, and with eyes still shut he tries to prolong the voluptuous vision as long as possible, to immortalise it perhaps.

dreams of a rape of nymphs

> 'These nymphs I would perpetuate.'

Meanwhile he opens his eyes, but the illusion of his dream is so strong that he still sees the luminous forms of the goddesses shimmering through shadows, partly due to his own sleep, partly to the motionless leafage over his head. And hence the doubt:

> 'Was it a dream I loved?'

But while the shades of sleep evaporate, the branches of

193

the trees persist — 'the true wood itself.' There is no more doubt. The Faun sees that he was alone, alas! and merely dreamed.

But his subtle spirit meditates a hypothesis. There were two nymphs in this dream. Who knows! Perhaps they were begotten of some error in his senses. The chaster one of the two had blue and cold eyes. Was she not suggested by 'the tinkling of a spring'? And the other, 'all sighs,' was not she on the contrary evoked by the touch of the breeze? No, the only tinkling in this wood is that of the flute which the Faun has been playing; and the only breeze perceptible is that of the inspiration which escapes from his double pipe and that one sees away there on the horizon where a summer haze mounts to rejoin the heaven whence it came.

There is nothing left then for the Faun but to abandon all further questioning and, following his own inspiration, to sing of his own dream.

'I was cutting reeds,' he says, 'to make a flute, when I saw on the water in the distance the undulation of an animal whiteness. At the first sound of my pipes these vague forms — are they swans? No, by Zeus! they are naiads! — take flight and disperse!'

Of this headlong flight nothing now subsists; nothing in the calm of this afternoon reveals the panic and flight of this troop of goddesses, too numerous to be taken by surprise, which disappeared the moment the naive musician gave the 'la' on his flute. Ah well!

194

since he is alone, he will get up and sing, bathed in the ancient light and like a lily for his ingenuousness.

As he rises the Faun feels on his breast what might be the memory of a bite. Perhaps he didn't dream? A bite! that would be a more convincing proof than a kiss, that 'sweet nothing' which evaporates at once. But alas! when he looks, his breast is 'virgin of proof.' Well, let's think no more about it. Only his flute knows the key to the enigma,[9] this flute which was once that nymph Syrinx and which now has but one dream, to amuse the youthful beauties around by a musical imitation of their forms: to transform softly — the voice as low as when one makes love — the sinuosities of thighs and backs (such as the Faun's inner vision traces behind his closed eyelids) into the undulations of a sonorous, monotonous line.[10]

'Try then, malicious Syrinx,' you who alone know how a nymph escapes us and 'vanishes' in music, try to flower again as a naiad of the lake. Meanwhile the Faun will content himself with memories and imaginary pleasures; just as when he has sucked grapes he blows up the empty skins and contemplates till evening the light shining through them, enjoying the illusion.

[9] 'Mystery,' 'arcane,' like that which Midas' barber once confided to a hole in the earth, and which was repeated by the reed.

[10] In French the construction here is: — Le jonc jumeau . . . qui rêve que (= qui voudrait que) nous amusions . . . et (qui rêve) de faire évanouir . . . de dos ou de flanc par (vus en songe) . . . une vaine, sonore et monotone ligne.

The story is taken up again and the Faun tells how, after the flight of the naiads, as he still pursued them, suddenly he found at his feet two nymphs asleep, mingled in a careless embrace, 'sleeping amid their casual arms.' He seizes the couple and carries them off, in the hope of a burning amour, towards a mass of roses. There in spite of their resistance he covers with kisses the bodies of the two goddesses, from the feet of the cruel one (all sighs none the less!) to the heart of the timid one (with eyes like cold springs). But alas! the anger of the Gods is aroused by seeing the ravishing Faun break in this way the embraces of the virgins, that 'dishevelled tangle of kisses' that they themselves 'kept so well commingled.' And at the moment when the Satyr was abandoning himself to more intimate pleasures, a sudden feebleness, 'a vague failing,' makes him loose his grasp. The two nymphs escape from him, both the burning virgin and the 'younger, naive one' whom he had held up till then by one of her fingers with a view to amorous education.

A long silence follows the recital. The end approaches, and when the poet begins again it is in a relaxed strain, but contented and already half somnolent. The Faun consoles himself by the thought of future delights. They will come inevitably. For, just as the purple flesh of pomegranates attracts swarms of bees, the blood of Fauns flows to appease the desires of goddesses. The Faun is given to boasting. He even flatters himself be-

196

forehand with the thought of a sensational rape. When the evening comes Venus descends, poses her white foot on the lava of Etna which sleeps and thundering dumbly lowers its flames. Yes, surely the Faun will ravish Venus. . . . What? he holds her already, her the queen of all nymphs; that will avenge him on the others:

'O penalty sure. . . .'

But the very exaggeration of the dream shows that the Faun is falling asleep again. Succumbing to the heat he stretches himself on the sand, opening his mouth — for wine, for sunshine? I know not which — both perhaps. Another silence, 'Adieu, Nymphs,' he says at last. He is going to plunge into sleep to find again that night wherein dreams float and dissolve, the shade wherein the couple of nymphs disappeared.

'Adieu, both! I shall see the shade you became.'

Note. — Debussy is said to have declared that in writing his admirable 'Prélude à l'après-midi d'un Faune' he followed the poem verse by verse. Certainly it is possible to find in the music the sleepy hesitations of the opening, the 'empty, sonorous, monotonous line' of the pipes, the flight of the naiads, the voluptuous ardour of the central scene, the scattering of the motive, the return to solitude, and finally the reversion to the unconsciousness of sleep.

SAINT [11]

This poem is perhaps one of the best that Mallarmé ever wrote, though it is seldom quoted. Its extraordinary tonal unity and the rigour of its symmetry, which in no way damages an exquisite sensibility (on the contrary, this is heightened), make it, to my mind, a masterpiece analogous to the most astonishing of the Italian Annunciations.

The verses are opposed to each other in two pairs. The sentence appearing to finish at the second quatrain returns, for the second panel of the diptych, by means of a simple apposition — 'At this monstrance window' of the ninth line repeating exactly the 'at this window' of the first. There are no difficulties in the style, except perhaps the use, familiar in Mallarmé, of the word 'flight' for 'wing' in line eleven; for obviously it is the angel's wing, shaped like a harp, that the saint brushes with her raised finger.

To the formal symmetry there corresponds a strict 'ordonnance' of the form.[12] The starting point of the poem, I imagine, must have been a figure in a stained-glass window. But the Saint seems to correspond, in

[11] The Saint is Sainte Cécile. The poem was presented to Mme. Cécile Brunet at Avignon.

[12] This obsolete term of the classical poetic gives M. Mauron's meaning far more clearly than alternatives, and the term is so useful that it might well be re-introduced. — Translator's note.

198

Mallarmé's thought, with the image of an ideal poetry, not human or capable of being realised, but, if I may use such a word, celestial. Human art, in the forms in which it preoccupied Mallarmé, namely, Music and Literature (the actual title of his lecture at Cambridge), is here represented in the two first verses by the lute and the book. But these are, for the Saint, instruments of the past, as appears from the symmetrically repeated word 'once.'

'Once with flute or mandola.'
'Once for vespers and complines.'

To this terrestrial art is opposed, in the second panel of the diptych, a celestial art. The 'window' becomes a 'monstrance window.' The instrument is an angel's wing. With her poised finger, the Saint seems to touch it delicately. She has become 'Musician of silence.' There can be no doubt, for any one who has recognised in Mallarmé's poetry the increasing importance of imaginations, whitenesses, absences, of 'nothing,' that this silence is the end of the scale of which I have written in the preface, the *non-existence* towards which all works of art are only transitions.

Let me also note, in considering the first verse, that the idea of ancient instruments (lute, clavichord, mandoline) and of soft music was always associated in Mallarmé's mind with that of chaste, and often ma-

199

ternal, femininity. On this subject, see *Gift of a Poem*: —

> 'And, your voice recalling viol and clavecin,
> With your faded finger you will press the breast
> Whence . . .'

So also in the sonnet 'A lace curtain stands effaced':

> 'Sadly sleeps a mandola
> Whose hollow void is musical
>
> Such that towards some window pane
> According to no womb but its
> Filial, one might be born.'

The similarity between this piece and *Saint* is striking.

A FUNERAL TOAST

The general idea of this poem is simple. '*Toast Funèbre*,' says Mallarmé in his Bibliography of 1898, 'comes from the composite work, the *Tombeau de Théophile Gautier, Maître et Ombre, à qui s'adresse l'invocation*.'[13] Théophile Gautier, an atheist like Mallarmé himself, did not believe in any life beyond the tomb. The toast is a profession of faith, or rather of absence of faith, and at the same time a protest against

[13] 'The Tomb of Théophile Gautier, Master and Shade to whom the invocation is addressed.'

any religious attempts to exploit the poet's memory. There may well have been at Gautier's death incidents to which Mallarmé apparently alludes, but at which we can only guess in our ignorance of the actual facts; perhaps a religious ceremony carried out in spite of the poet's wishes, spiritualistic evocations, who knows what?

The detail of the poem being rather complex and often obscure, I shall try to give a commentary almost line by line. I feel as much as any one a certain shame at paraphrasing in prose a beautiful poem. A blasphemy perhaps, but a necessary blasphemy. It would be absurd to deny the difficulty of the text. All that I ask is that, the elucidation once completed, the reader should return at once to the poem alone.

l. 1. 'Oh, thou (Théophile Gautier) emblem of our happiness which is purely terrestrial ('fatal' because it is terminated by death).'

ll. 3, 4. Do not think that I offer my empty cup, where a monster of gold suffers,[14] to the magic hope of seeing you appear some day a spectre wandering in a corridor.

l. 2. Such a health would be a health to madness and this libation would be a blank libation.

l. 5. I cannot be content with such a derisory 'hope.'

[14] What is this monster of gold? I do not know. Poetry, perhaps. The cup engraved with a monster is the symbol of St. John. But has this any connection with the poem?

l. 6. I have put you myself into the tomb.

ll. 7, 8. The torches are extinguished against the doors of the tomb.

ll. 9, 10, 11. And I know, elected as I am for our simple feast which celebrates 'the absence of the poet,' that this fair monument contains him altogether.

ll. 12, 13, 14, 15. Something, however, emerges from the monument when the setting sun illuminates the window (of the tomb): its light is reflected back to our mortal (pagan) sun.

And this is a kind of symbol: Gautier loved pagan nature; he sang it with passion, gloriously cultivating his craft (l. 12); he continued it up to the moment of 'vile and common' death, and it seems that by this reflexion of light he returns to the sun what it gave.

ll. 16, 17. The 'false pride of men' trembles to declare itself (l. 17), unlike the *true* pride which is 'magnificent, total and solitary' (l. 16).

ll. 18, 19. This 'haggard' (fearful) crowd proclaims that we shall become spectres like to ourselves, admitting thus that they are now like the spectres that they will be, with only this sad difference that they are now opaque.

ll. 20, 21. But as for me I have scorned to give way to tears which would have been horrible even though they did not deprive me of my lucidity. Tears which are themselves physically 'lucid,'

being in fact embroidered in silver on the funeral
hangings covering the 'vain walls' of the church
during the ceremony.

l. 23. 'When . . .': here occurs an allusion to some
unknown occurrence. Was it a religious hope to
which one of the mourners gave expression? Or
can it be that 'the virgin hero of the posthumous
hope' is simply a Catholic priest? Mallarmé
might have seen him at the funeral, with down-
cast eyes ('blind') 'proud and speechless.' His
sacerdotal robes are compared to a vague shroud.
This hypothesis would explain 'transmuted itself'
thus: — The mass of men, 'the haggard crowd,'
believes in the future spectre, but therefrom 'one
of the passers-by' detaches himself, and becomes
thereby the protagonist of the crowd, 'the virgin
hero.' But I must leave it to the reader to decide
on this point.

ll. 27-31. The lines which follow are not much clearer.
I propose the following explanation. The religious
words which Gautier did *not* utter (l. 27) imply
a belief, an appeal to Nothingness. He who refuses to believe in God can only believe in
nothingness, and sees at once this vast Gulf
hollow up, impetuously ('irascible') as if, in our
cosmogony, there opened a vast hollow through
which an 'irascible' wind rushes.

And nothingness once admitted, an inevitable

question arises: 'If there is no God, what then is real? what then is the earth?' At the moment of death, and perhaps after death, when Théophile Gautier was already a 'man who had ceased,' Nothingness must have yelled this question to him as to all who refuse to believe in some divinity; and the poet already ceasing to exist, already dissolving into space which makes a 'plaything' of his answer, makes the only answer possible for an atheist: 'I do not know.'

ll. 32–35. The Master, by the depth of his intelligence, has spread around him this doctrine, and appeased the 'disquieting' anxiety of men on the subject of a possible future life. The idea of an Eden (an earthly Paradise) has always haunted men's imaginations under different forms — but the last meaning given it by the Poet (the last quiver) evokes only a kind of ideal garden, where spiritual flowers would grow — not roses and lilies, but the Rose and the Lily, those ideal flowers which Mallarmé in his *Divagations* describes as 'absent from all bouquets.' That which the word 'Eden' retains of mystery ('the mystery of a name') applies to this unreal Garden, the only Paradise to which we can lay claim (l. 35).

ll. 36 *et seq.* But the future life is an error; does nothing then remain of Gautier? — 'Forget so sombre a creed.' The Genius is all light ('without

shade' in both senses of the word). But, says
Mallarmé, I will answer your desire and tell you
what survives of the Poet — his poetical ideas.
He has accomplished the duty of genius: he has
transmuted the flowers of our earthly gardens
into ideal flowers. And it is these that I see surviving so that the 'calm disaster' of an earthly
death should not be without honour (l. 43).
These ideas, at once words and flowers, cause a
solemn agitation in the air (l. 44), and the
poet's look resting on them, this look as clear as
'rain and diamonds,' 'isolates' (traces the contour of) their forms in the luminous space. None
of them fades because ideas are incorruptible
(l. 47). These gardens, this 'boscage' are our
true 'sojourn,' and the poet has the 'humble and
grand' function of banishing thence the dream
and religious sentimentality which would mist
over their luminous reality (l. 50).

'So that' the Poet attains this end, that the
morning after his death, when the day rises in the
cemetery (l. 51), ancient (pagan) death being
only, as it was for Gautier, to keep the eyes and
mouth closed, we may see by the alley the 'solid
tomb' wherein is imprisoned all evil: 'both
grudging silence' (kept by the closed mouth) and
'oppressive night' (kept by the closed eyes).

Thus the ill is restrained within the tomb

whilst the good (light and words) live on in the earthly or spiritual garden.

PROSE POUR DES ESSEINTES

The 'proses' — prosae — were religious works written in that decadent Latin in which rhyme appears for the first time in the language. *La Prose pour des Esseintes* is so called because of the extraordinary 'richness' of the rhymes [15] each of which is in fact a play upon words. 'Gloire du long désir, Idées . . . La famille des iridées . . .'

A poet and a young woman have slept by the water-side. Waking up, the poet says that he has been in an island of enormous flowers. She replies that there is no island. He insists: yes there is an island and we both went there. Such would seem to be the story. Mallarmé gives it a symbolic meaning. He maintains that the platonic world of ideas exists, he has been there; but he returned because these highflying journeys are dangerous to the mind, the flowers grew so great that the poet feared for his reason.

[15] The 'rime riche' has no exact counterpart in English. It is a rhyme in which the initial consonant of the last syllable, or of several syllables as above, is repeated. *Translator.*

'— de lis multiples la tige
   Grandissait trop pour nos raisons' [16]

'I fled from that place', says the poet for fear of
going mad; 'but that certainly does not mean that it does
not exist!' 'Et non, comme pleure la rive . . . que ce
pays n'exista pas.' The wise and gentle sister ('soeur
sensée et tendre') urges departure and a resurrection
into life ('Anastase') lest beauty ('pulchérie') give way
to insanity ('le trop grand glaïeul'). Mallarmé has given
up the flight of the imagination ('hyperbole'), which
was an absolute leap into the unknown, in order to return to that business of patient scrawling in which the
world of the supernatural becomes a map, the idea of
flowers a dried specimen of the herbarium, and ecstasy a
simple ritual. The imaginative leap into the absolute,
the triumphant soaring, are definitely things of the past
('Hyperbole, de ma memoire — triomphalement ne
sais-tu te lever . . .') We are back at 'l'oeuvre de
patience.'

Let us now examine the poem stanza by stanza.

1. Flight of the imagination, supreme truth, you no
longer arise triumphant from my memory. Truth is now
shut in an iron book ('livre de fer').

2. For now, in order to rediscover the Idea ('hymne des

[16] ". . . j'ai presque perdu la raison et ce sens des paroles les
plus familières." Letter to Coppée, April 1868.

coeurs spirituels') I must toil patiently [17] working upon material things ('atlas, herbiers et rituels').

3. We two walked together breathing the scent of the flowers.

4, 5. Authority is undone (authority in general and masculine authority in particular) if we are to be told by those who understand (i.e. by the wise and gentle sister) that this sunlit landscape (which we saw in our common dream) is nameless, that it is not clear as noonday, in fact that it is nowhere under the sun — when all the time a hundred irises grow and bear witness to it.

6, 7. But yes, in an island which was real, although ideal, every flower silently increased (by force of imagination); each was infinite ('immenses') and distinct — as is the case with ideas.

8. The sense is clear. The acrobatic rhyme 'des iridées' is probably the psychological origin of 'cent-iris.' The rhyme 'voir . . . devoir' reappears in *Toast Funèbre*.

9. But while Adam rejoiced Eve cast down her eyes and smiled that smile which Adam is forever trying to understand ('comme à l'entendre-tel qu'à l'entendre').

[17] It was from this patient work, which he then found too hard that Mallarmé wished to escape before 1870. He now accepts 'le devoir idéal que nous font les jardins de cet astre.' The flowers of *Toast Funèbre* are evidently the same ideal flowers as those of the *Prose*.

10. What then was behind the dispute ('litige')? [18] The fact that the flight of fancy is mixed with madness; looking at so many ideal and infinitely expanding flowers one loses one's poor human wits and one's sense of reality.

> '. . . de lis multiples la tige
> Grandissait *trop* pour nos raisons'

11, 12. So be it, but it is no use pretending *now*, after the dream, as the sea or the river pretends, that there is no isle, that the wide landscape is empty, that the ideal country does not exist. The words may be rearranged thus: (le litige n'était pas) tel que le dit la rivière pleurarde, quand elle s'obstine, monotonement, à vouloir que — dans mon étonnement ingénu à ouïr le flot qui s'écarte attester sans fin sur mes pas le ciel et la carte — arrive cette ample evidence (ampleur): que ce pays n'exista pas.

12, 13. The two final stanzas bring the tale lightly to an end. The lady puts a stop to the siesta and to the story of the dream. 'Up,' she says. Ideally this means that she renounces her part in the ideal garden ('abdique son extase') and throws herself into a new life (Resurrection-Anastasis). But he who comes back to life leaves a grave behind him somewhere. Where? Nowhere to be sure ('sous aucun climat'). And the tomb bears the name

[18] 'Oh sache l'Esprit de litige: O que l'Esprit de litige sache donc.'

'beauty' ('Pulchérie') hidden, by a pleasantry characteristic of the entire poem — behind a flower of the
imagination, 'le trop grand glaïeul.'

EVENTAIL DE MADAME MALLARMÉ

1. The birth of the poem: still unformed the coming
verse emerges like an insect from its chrysalis. The poet
sees it as nothing more than a vague rhythm, a beating
of wings, which is for the present its only means of expression.

2. Now this fan, with its own mute rhythm appears as
the silent herald of the poem,[19] if indeed it is the fan
whose flutter is reflected in the mirror behind Madame
Mallarmé.

   (Mallarmé often describes a poem as an apparition in
the glass. The fan, through its reflection, becomes a
wing which precedes and announces the poem, it is a
silent messenger, 'Aile tout bas la courrière.')

3. The word 'limpide' naturally describes the mirror.
It is there that the poem is made. How? Every wing
beat carries a feather of flying ash which the poet must
collect. Mallarmé frequently compares poetic thought
to a casting of ashes in which the words are the ashes. Cf.

---

[19] Cf. *Hommage* à Vasco. (Page 114)

> 'Ci-gît le noble vol humain
> Cendre ployée avec les livres'

and again:

> 'Maint rêve vespéral brûlé par le phénix
> Que ne recueille pas de cinéraire amphore.'

In short the general idea is this: The beating of Madame Mallarmé's fan announces the poem; looking past her the poet thinks that he can discern the shape of the verses that he will write.

ANOTHER FAN

Belonging to Mademoiselle Mallarmé

This poem is spoken by the fan. A curiously subtle fan, since it knows what is perhaps the secret of all aesthetic, how to refuse Life, lie to reality, and not respond to an exterior stimulus by the appropriate response, but, having reached the threshold of action, to stop, laughing at the universal deception, and play or contemplate rather than act. Man is an artist in so far as he can stop living. As a painter he draws, rather than embraces, the nude. Poet, he gathers not fruit but images. Or so at least thought the Faun, whose pipe 'turns the cheek's trouble to itself.' So also thinks the fan. Being winged, as its movement shows, it should have known the real pleasures of flight. But, since it is an artist, it knows better. If the dreamer's hand can hold and imprison this flight, it will plunge into the space of pure imagination. For as soon as one lies to life, one enters the platonic kingdom of Ideas, of Not-being.

> 'Dear dreamer, that I may plunge
> Into pure trackless delight,
> Know, by a subtle deceit,
> How to keep my wing in your hand.'

So the game begins. The emprisoned fan goes through the motions of flight. But instead of serving in some useful progress, each movement of the wing only serves to open, dilate and reclose the space before the young woman's face — without any object except the pleasure of the motion.

> 'Vastness!'

An immense space comes into being when the horizon under the fan draws back — it comes into being, but for no one. Nothing really happens; if any happiness were possible, it would not happen. The girl's lips, uncovered by the fan, suggest a kiss, but there is no one to kiss them. The excitement of the imagination arises from just these checks on the threshold of action. And, when the fan recloses, shy happiness, a happiness which flies reality, like a laugh which is checked and becomes internal, flows and glides along the converging folds of the fan, closing like a folded wing. This is the game; all idea of power is banished from it. It gives no real control over the actual world. But it opens up, to any one who plays it, the territories of imagination, the shores of non-existence, those which 'stagnate on the gold' of twilight. The folded fan is the sceptre of these. The final couplet closes the poem with the fixity of a scintillation immobile as the contemplator.

DAME — SANS TROP D'ARDEUR . . .

The poet describes his feelings on the occasion of the anniversary of a peaceful love affair (with Méry Laurent), tenderly peaceful it is true, and changed to an uneventful friendship ('mué en amitié monotone').

'Chaque année' — each year of this attachment returns without having brought any sentimental crisis, without any burning summer of passion — 'Sans trop d'ardeur à la fois.' These are the two essential terms of the sentence from which the sonnet is made; one must perceive the connection in order to understand the syntactical construction. The quatrains, beginning with 'sans trop d'ardeur,' express that which the year, or rather, the anniversary, has failed to give to the lovers; the tercets show what it *has* brought.

1–6. There has been no excess of passion such as that which incarnadines a rose ('. . . enflammant — La rose'), no dramatic frenzies, wounds, agonies, tears, storms or those spells of clear weather which follow the storm.

Verse 3 contains the most daring of ellipses. The line must be understood as: 'lasse même du blanc habit, en dénoue les lacets de pourpre.'

Verse 4 describes the dew sparkling in the deepest, the most carnal depths of an opened flower. It is difficult to say so much in so few words. Verses 5 and 6 are in an ironic mood, which is never very far away in Mallarmé; no histrionics, no, not even that rather chilly weather which follows the storm, even that would be too eventful.

Verses 7 and 8 mark the transition. It is understood now that each year will pass by without romantic exaltation. Nevertheless the years seem bent on enlarging the sphere of everyday tenderness ('Jalouse d'apporter je ne sais quel espace — Au simple jour le jour très vrai du sentiment').

How does this happen? Simply enough say the tercets; these are new years of a kind that show no alteration in a charming face. The anniversary comes round like the gentle agitation of a fan in a room in which the fresh air of passion has been replaced by a mild and peaceful atmosphere. That tiny gale is sufficient to provoke just the slight emotion that is needed.

SONNET: O si chère de loin.

Ist Quatrain. The image of his absent mistress is so vivid in Mallarmé's imagination that he thinks that he can detect her perfume; it is as though a memory of flowers was suspended above an empty crystal vase.

Mallarmé frequently uses the words 'baumes,' or 'aromates' when speaking of the scent of a headdress. He has in mind the idea of some very ancient perfume and with it is associated the idea of time as also of flowers. Cf. 'Quelle soie aux baumes de temps' — this in relation to Méry and her hair and, in another context: 'De l'essence ravie aux vieillesses — des roses.'

2nd Quatrain. Here we find the rose which Mallarmé always associates with Méry. Cf. 'Victorieusement fui le suicide *beau*.'

> 'Comme un casque guerrier d'impératrice enfant
> Dont pour te figurer il tomberait des roses.'

Here it is not the person but the smile, that smile which Mallarmé believed that he had always known, of which he speaks. It opens out, literally embalmed, looking down on past and future alike, as a flower looks down upon the vase in which it stands.

The Tercets. The mistress appears as an ideal creature, as a sister —for Mallarmé there is no more tender form of endearment. Nevertheless his memories remind him of a very different kind of sweetness, less fraternal than erotic.

REMÉMORATION D'AMIS BELGES

The idea is simple: walking through Bruges with new friends, it seems to Mallarmé that the age-worn patina of the buildings dignifies his friendship, a friendship that would otherwise be too new an emotion. It is a poetical translation of the common phrase: 'it seems as though I had always known you.'

The difficulties arise from the absence of punctuation and from the oddity of the metaphor when pushed to its utmost material details.

The construction: the sonnet is made of one sentence. The beginning may be reconstructed thus: 'A des heures et sans que tel souffle émeuve la pierre — toute la vétusté, presque couleur encens, étant furtive d'elle (quittant furtivement la pierre) et visible — je sens qu'elle se dévêt pli à pli, flotte, etc.' The notion of stones clothed in a veil of patina, a widow's veil ('un voile de veuve') which is suddenly to be removed, is to be avoided. On the contrary the stone itself is, as it were, made of successive layers of age which fall away one by one ('pli selon pli') and melt into thin air, thus forming a kind of aroma, a witness of antiquity, which spreads its influence over the new and sudden friendship — 'sur la soudaineté de notre amitié neuve.' The image is of course ridiculous if factually examined; it needs the vague exactitudes of the poet's words (*'vètusté, couleur encens, furtive, flotte'*) to make it acceptable. The third verse of the second quatrain is a kind of parenthesis. 'Notre amitié neuve (à) nous, immémoriaux quelques-uns si contents,' must be understood as: 'nous, quelques hommes immémorialement ensemble et si contents.' 'Immémoriaux' does not qualify 'nous,' but 'quelques-uns' — through all eternity we few together.

The end of the second quatrain needs a comma; the sentence continues with a splendid image of a flight of swans in the dawn ('une aube multipliée sous forme de cygnes'), then follows the hommage of the last tercet '. . . Quand cette cité m'apprit solennellement lesquels de ses fils un autre vol (another flight than that of the swans and the morning — that of time) désigne pour irradier l'esprit ainsi qu'une aile prompte.'

CHANSONS BAS

These are short humorous verses — asides. They and their titles are such as might be intended to accompany engravings.[19a]

[19a] Cf. *La Bibliographie de l'édition de* 1898. 'Chansons bas I & II commentent, avec divers quatrains, dans le recueil *Les Types de Paris*, les inspirations du Maître-peintre Raffaëlli, qui les inspira et les accepta.'

I. LE SAVETIER

Despair of the poet before this honest artisan who knows nothing beyond his trade, as a soldier knows nothing beyond his duty. It is no use trying to draw him out ('Hors de la poix rien à faire').

Everyone is what he is: 'Le lys naît blanc.' Tastes differ, that is all, and one may like a flower better than a cobbler. The 'rime riche' plays an essential part in producing the comic effect — and this often explains the apparently haphazard construction of these verbal arabesques. Quite apart from the colour contrast it is well worth while to construct a jigsaw pattern between the cobblers wax and the lily and thus to make 'Comme odeur' rhyme with 'raccomodeur.'

The Chinese irony of the rest of the poem, with its antithesis between the poet's longing for bare heels — 'un besoin de talons nus' and the implacable thickness of soles — 'plus de cuir que je n'eus jamais' — which the shoemaker sticks on regardless of what anyone may say, is clear enough. And to crown everything he offers to make yet another pair of shoes.

> 'Il recréerait des souliers,
> O pieds! si vous le vouliez.'

II. LA MARCHANDE D'HERBES AROMATIQUES

A verminous gypsy woman offers bunches of lavender to be hung on the walls of water closets — 'de lieux les absolus lieux.' The poet rejects this 'hypocrisy.' The only possible reconstruction of lines 7 and 8 would seem to be: 'Pour quelle ventre qui se raille renaisse aux sentiments bleus.' He tells the hawker that she would do better to put the lavender in her hair as a scent, or as love token.

The poems which follow require no explanation.

BILLET A WHISTLER

As is explained in the *Bibliographie de l'édition de 1898*, this is a poetic comment on the title of an English periodical, *The Whirlwind*, 'envers qui Whistler fut princier.' It is in fact a reply to the question: 'What is this whirlwind?' It is not a dust storm of the streets, says Mallarmé, but the whirlwind of the dance.

The despised squalls ('rafales méprisées') of the first quatrain would seem to describe the usual gossip of the satirical journals. The kind of thing which blows a man's hat away, the common joke of the funny man. *The Whirlwind* claims that it devotes itself to more serious matters. The winds which blow through its pages are set up by a sylphide, or rather, by an ideal dance, 'celle même dont nous vécûmes.' It is a wind of the spirit, at once playful and imperious. Its aim is (simply) to blow down everything ('tout foudroyer'), everything being trite except Whistler himself — '. . . tout, hormis lui, rebattu.' It shall be done without sparing anybody, and without anger; but the greatest care shall be taken that Whistler himself shall remain unruffled by the lightest breeze.

RONDELS

Of these two gallantries addressed to Méry Laurent the first is amusing largely on account of the grammatical subtlety with which the theme is treated. A beauty wakes up, and thoughts and memories of yesterday come to light in her mind. What then does she remember? Nothing that does not make her pout, a pout which becomes even more cruel if it is followed by a laugh. In fact nothing has happened, not a breath, not a memory remains to give one a clue. The third stanza describes the freshness of her face and the brilliance of her eyes. The construction is: 'Tous les rêves (émerveillés quand cette beauté les déjoue) ne produisent rien, fleur sur la joue, dans l'œil diamants impayés, que vous n'ayez au réveil.'

The subject of *Rondel II* is clear enough. It describes a smile and a kiss in silence. 'Cette rose ne l'interromps' unites two images: the interruption of the kiss, the tearing apart of the rose formed by two joined lips. 'Jamais de chants' — no song, ever, melts and sparkles as swiftly as a smile. Silent, silent (twice silent and both silent) the kiss, hidden between joined lips like a mantled nymph ('sylphe dans la pourpre d'empire') is broken suddenly when a wing-tipped smile appears. Here the curve of the lips has suggested a cherub's wing — 'Un baiser flambant se déchire — Jusqu'aux pointes des ailerons.'

LITTLE AIR

The most complicated and tiresome explanations have been given of this short piece. Its undeniable difficulty arises from a singular impressionist method. The *Little Airs* are, even more than the other poems, occasional works — notes of a state of mind, a change of humour, a fugitive thought: they can only be enjoyed if we take account of the exact conditions which gave rise to them. But these exact conditions, very real for Mallarmé, are only known to us by allusions.

Here, however, it seems easy enough to reconstitute them; and no doubt, as I have noted in the preface, it would be useless, poetically, to make more precise what remains dubious. Mallarmé, in the company of a mistress, finds himself at sunset on the bank of a river. The young woman is going to bathe. Mallarmé looks at the landscape, characterless and deserted; this is the first impression:

'Just a solitude.'

His look discovers nothing of what had been the charm of past walks; here there is no swan, no quay. I must return later to this unexpected thought because nothing in the text, at first sight, explains it. This leaves it to be supposed that Mallarmé, for some reason, only perceives the uninteresting horizon of river and bank. Perhaps he is lying in his favourite boat, that of the 'Nénuphar Blanc.' I must ask the reader to imagine the landscape, the river, the empty curve of the bank, and, overhead, the sky. It is in fact the sky which has ceased to interest the poet. The gold of the sunset has painted it in such violent streaks of colour, with such an affectation of glory,[20] that Mallarmé has turned away from it — a genuine 'abdication' — to reflect simply on the abandonment, the 'unusedness' (the real sense of 'desuetude') of the bank.

Suddenly two things happen, almost simultaneously. First, a bird, apparently a white bird, gets up, flies skimming the surface, 'languidly' slides along the curve of the river ('coasts'), or rather, as the eye follows the bird, the curve of the river appears to follow its flight; that, at least to my mind, is the only possible syntax, the whole piece being a single sentence with 'solitude' as the common subject of the two verbs 'mirrors' and 'coasts.' To cut the sentence in half by a full stop after the second quatrain, giving 'a shy bird' as subject of 'coasts,' would

[20] Compare the similar irony of *Victoriously fled is the grand suicide* where the sunset is called a 'puerile triumph.' (Page 103)

222

involve making the latter a verb without a complement, a grammatical form impossible in French.

Secondly, the bather dives. The construction is 'If your nude jubilation, exulting beside (me or the bird) plunges into the billow become you.'

The two events are doubtless related; the sudden movement of the diver has startled the bird. But the poet's mind, readily turning towards metaphor, creates a more curious relation between them. The white gliding flight of the bird, following a curve of the landscape, is like the final action of slipping off the shift which languidly sweeps the curves of a woman's body. A forced and far-fetched comparison in most contexts, here of the keenest appropriateness. If, from this point, you follow word by word the six last lines you will see that the syntax has not been complicated at random; the order of the words is that of the divers movements. First she undresses:

> 'Languidly coasts
> Like white linen doffed.'

Then the shift flies away, or rather the bird, whose flight suggests the shift, since the poet seems to have turned his back on the young woman undressing:

> 'Some shy bird . . .'

And followed by the immediate dive:

> '. . . if plunges.'

The double exultation of the jump and of the jet of foam:

> 'Exulting beside.'

The diver disappearing, confused with the water:

> 'In the billows become you.'

Finally, in the water, the reappearance, laughing and waving her arms, of the diver's naked body:

> 'Your nude jubilation.'

The disappearance of the diver in the river reinforces strongly the preceding metaphor; the bird glides along the stream like a shift over a body, and then, emphasising the point, body and river are confused together. The most curious effect of all is that this impression of whiteness gliding along a curve brings us back, in the subtlest fashion, to the swan and quay of the opening — indeed this constitutes the only poetic justification of a regret that is, to say the least of it, bizarre. Why, of all pleasant river landscapes, regret that one in particular? Because there is something here which recalls it. This also explains the 'But' of line nine; there is not, apparently, swan or quay in the actual landscape, but there occurs something to replace them; a bird, a whiteness, and languorous, stroking movement.

One of the most beautiful works and one of the most obscure — a rapid transition from reality to non-existence, from sound to silence, a single rubato phrase rocketting and falling in showers . . . It reminds one of Chopin. The subject is a song — that of the nightingale let us say — rising suddenly to a height which is not only unheard of, but unheard, bursting — as one may say — into silence; the effort has been so great that the musician may die of it.[21]

It is perhaps worthwhile to reconstruct the first two quatrains. 'L'oiseau qu'on n'ouït jamais une autre fois en la vie (voix étrangère au bosquet et par nul écho suivie) a dû, indomptablement, comme s'y lance mon espoir, éclater, perdu, là-haut, avec furie et silence.' Foreign ('étrangère') because the grove is usually filled with the sound of audible and intelligible voices. The voice of the stranger in the grove is naturally that which speaks of other things, that which gives 'un sens plus pur aux mots de la tribu.'[22]

After this burst of fury and silence there comes an organ point, a disquieting transition, a dreadful sob, worse than all other sobs — beyond everything ('sanglot

---

[21] 'Car voici le miracle de chanter. On se projette, haut, comme va le cri.' — *Divagations.*
[22] *Le Tombeau d'Edgar Poe.*

pire'); and one does not know whether it really came
from the musician or from the listener.

The construction would seem to be: 'Le hagard
musicien, dans le doute, expire cela; le pire sanglot
a-t-il jailli de mon sein ou du sien? — déchiré va-t-il
rester sur quelque sentier?'

PETIT AIR (GUERRIER)

This work appeared in 1895 as an epigraph to an
article in *La Revue Indépendante* which will be found
in *Divagations* under the title of *L'Action Restreinte*.

The poem expresses a single desire: 'leave me alone.'
Enough of these visitors, sympathetic though they are,
who come asking me how to make changes in one's
social environment. Away with these importunate in-
vaders. Mallarmé, sitting by his fireside, sees the glow
redden his trousers, clothing him in a scarlet uniform
which suits his bellicose mood nicely. The irony of the
poem lends itself to acrobatic prosody: 'hormis l'y
taire — militaire' is simply a joke rhyme. All the rest
is perfectly clear if one replaces the stops.

Je guette l'invasion, brandis ma baguette

Nue ou d'écorce tenace,
Pas pour battre le Teuton
Mais comme une autre menace
(A la fin que me veut-on?)

De trancher ras cette ortie
Folle de la sympathie.

WHEN THE SHADOW MENACED WITH
ITS FATAL LAW

Primacy of the spirit over the material universe, an un-
limited but senseless mass, is the Pascalian subject of
this poem. In reading it one inevitably thinks of Pascal's
famous phrase, 'L'homme n'est qu'un roseau . . . mais
c'est un roseau pensant.' [23] Mallarmé, like Pascal, contemplates the infinitude of the heavens, the multitude
of stars. But they do not cause in him the same fearful
emotion. For 'space — let it grow or grow less,' — perhaps a direct allusion to Pascal's double infinity — remains always 'like to itself.' To be quite frank this
immensity is uninteresting, and the innumerable stars
that 'roll' amid this 'ennui' are only 'vile fires,' simple
'witnesses' of the flowering of the spirit which may occur
here and there in the Universe, on the earth for instance.

This revolt of the human spirit against a Universe
which seems ready to crush it is the theme of many
philosophers, for it is difficult not to accept some form
of idealism when we reflect that all our knowledge takes
shape in a spirit. Thus one arrives almost inevitably at
an anthropocentric exaltation. Pascal found in God the

[23] 'Man is only a reed . . . but a reed that thinks.'

counterpoise to this pretension: 'S'il (l'homme) s'élève je l'abaisse. . . .' [24] Mallarmé, atheist as he was, asked later on the same service from Chance. Chance is greater than any possible actuality, stronger than any throw of the dice — now, 'all thought sends forth a throw of dice' — consequently Chance is stronger than any thought. By this means the 'Genius of the Earth' is put back into its place. But when Mallarmé wrote this sonnet he would seem not yet to have reached this level of ironical equilibrium. He exalts the human spirit without calling in any counterpoise. He exalts it all the more in that he himself has lost all hope of a future life; 'dazzled by his (new) faith,' he transfers to the human spirit a religious fervour which his atheism deprived of any object.

From this point of view the Sonnet becomes clear.

1st Quatrain. The 'ancient Dream' is the religious dream, our ancient longing for immortality, which torments man in his profoundest instincts ('my spine's desire and ill'). The Poet having lost his faith, this dream has also been menaced by death according to its 'fatal law.' Hitherto this dream has filled the heavens with its 'indubitable wing' which is now 'folded' in death — for the heavens have closed down like the ceiling of a tomb ('The funereal ceiling').

In the 2nd Quatrain Mallarmé has evidently before him the spectacle of a starry night (he says it directly

[24] 'If man raises himself, I abase him. . . .'

in the Sestet). He has just been comparing the heavens to black ceilings. A new image here arises. What was this Universe according to the ancient cosmogony? The mansion of God. A luxurious 'ebony hall' where God (its King) reigned, and on the walls of which the constellations ('famous garlands') die in strange contortions ('twist in their death'). But this ancient cosmogony afforded only a deceptive pride, as the solitary now sees it 'dazzled by his (new) faith' in the human spirit.

Sestet. Infinitely great or infinitely small, space remains insignificant. Only the spirit throws a light — that is the reason why the Earth 'sheds the glow of a rare mystery.' The Sonnet closes then like a picture of the Nativity. All the immense but stupid Universe surrounds the chosen star where there has just been lighted a mysterious illumination.

THIS VIRGIN, BEAUTIFUL AND LIVELY DAY

Of all Mallarmé's short pieces, this sonnet, *The Swan*, is perhaps the best known. It attracts attention first by its astonishing tonal unity, its accumulation of whitenesses and frosty glitter — 'virgin, lively, hard lake, frost, transparent glacier, swan, sterile winter, ennui, white agony, fantom, brightness, stilled, cold dream, useless exile.' No poet has ever accumulated in fourteen lines so many frosty syllables, so many overtones of the words 'winter' and 'white.'

Technically this tonal unity is reinforced in the French by the almost obsessional persistence of a single alliteration, the short cold 'i's' of the rhymes shine through the whole sonnet like icicles. Simply from the verbal point of view *The Swan* is a success; this alone is enough to give a poem a certain importance in literary history.

Another cause of its relative popularity is that the poem is evidently symbolical in general intention, and any cultivated person can at any rate see the general drift of it. The solitary swan, imprisoned in an icy landscape, evokes at once the artist in his 'ivory tower,' his estrangement from the world, his 'icy dream of contempt,' his boredom, his useless purity, and, too often, his sterility. We are in the (apparently) well-known region of 'art for art's sake'; there is a tradition of this sort of symbolism, and the reader feels himself less lost than in most Mallarméan landscapes. But if we wish to understand the sonnet — that is, to see what it may have signified to Mallarmé himself — we should be well advised not to adopt in a hurry any such conventional and emptied symbolism. One fact at any rate should suggest a doubt. The traditional artist in his ivory tower is a voluntary prisoner, despising the external world. The swan, in the poem, only thinks of escaping from the surrounding purity; he is immobilised against his will, cursing the cruelty of his exile. The symbolism of the poem is almost certainly less banal and more bitter than one might think at first sight. It is more likely to be about Mallarmé himself than the artist in general. The familiar air of the poem is deceptive. Before attempting the secondary sense of a poem it is necessary to understand its primary sense, which can only be done by a long and intimate acquaintance with the individual poet and poem.

The sonnet begins with a great beating of wings, or rather with a hope of flight. It is a fine, blue, frosty winter's morning, with a feeling in the air of excitement and impatience:

> 'This virgin, beautiful and lively day
> Will it tear with a stroke of its drunken wing
> The hard, forgotten lake . . .'

The lines express a hope of thaw and deliverance. But for the time being the swan is a prisoner, and the transparent ice, under a thin layer of hoar-frost, reflects the feathers of the bird, 'the flights unflown' (a somewhat ghostly reflection, whence the word 'haunts'). The two last lines of the quatrain are among the most beautiful Mallarmé ever wrote; they paint with impressionist precision the glassy, dull light of the reflection under the hoar-frost, and the spectral and unreal tonality is reinforced by the use of the abstract 'flights' for wings (see also, for this, *Another Fan*, page 97) and by the negation of 'which have not flown.' The use of such negations is one of the major discoveries of Mallarmé's technique; he is able to reinforce an effect of whiteness and pallor by the even greater pallor of not-being. He does the same thing in *Herodias:*

> 'Oh mirror!
> A cold water frozen with ennui in your frame,
> How often, for how long, unvisited
> Of dreams, and seeking my remembrances which are
> Like leaves beneath your ice's profoundness
> I to myself appeared a far-off shade.'

At this point a question occurs: how was the swan held prisoner? What prevented his flying? I remember an amusing discussion on this point between two 'Mallarméans,' the first holding that the starting-point of the poem was a swan whose wings had been clipped. 'The bird,' he said, 'is walking on the ice in a melancholy fashion, accompanied by the reflection of his useless wings.' But the other disputant maintained that the swan was actually frozen into the ice. 'Otherwise, what good would the thaw do him? What would it matter to him whether or not "the beautiful day" "tears the lake"? Don't you see that in the first tercet the bird tries to shake off the agony only by moving his neck, but that he can't walk?' 'That may be true,' replied the first, 'but in the first quatrain the word "haunts" seems to suggest movement.' 'Not necessarily.' For my own part, I find the first hypothesis more natural, and the second closer to the text. But the question is not of great importance. The 'beautiful day' arouses in the swan a hope of escape, and escape is in fact impossible, *why* does not matter. Perhaps, fundamentally, only because the swan is white:

'Fantom that to this place his brightness assigns him.'

Such poetic necessities have, in poetry, more importance than any practical contingency.

The second quatrain is syntactically very concentrated, and even (in French) incorrect. Moreover, the sense of the last two lines provides a new puzzle; the bird, apparently, has not migrated to a warmer climate before winter, whereas the swan is a northern bird, and cannot be considered not at home in a winter landscape. In fact it seems to be a matter of the opposition of 'sing' and 'live' to the 'stérile ennui' of frost and snow.

Thus, little by little, the beating wings of the opening are fixed, held and crystallised. It is this death of an effort, this contraction of hope, this retreat towards the immobility imposed by the environment, which is the real subject of the poem. The effort and the environment can be almost anything. The sonnet, like a piece of music, is a movement which can be found in many real situations and which can give rise to numerous imaginations. Essentially, it represents an unsuccessful

attempt at escape, the repression of a revolt by surroundings that impose themselves as an obsession. The first
quatrain leaps up, and then falls back, before a negation
and a ghost. In the second quatrain the movement is
taken up again, weaker, a simple escape into the past,
and the sterile winter returns. The protest of the first
tercet is only the movement of the bird's head and neck,
shaking off the snow and frost, fallen from the upper air
which no longer exists for him, and which he 'denies'
by ceasing to move. By the second tercet there is total
immobility, the spectral whiteness, winter, cold and
silence are triumphant. With their triumph the sonnet
closes, 'the poem ends, whiteness returns,' as Mallarmé
says elsewhere. This cold, which little by little freezes
the poem, is no doubt the final silence.

White was always for Mallarmé a synonym for
sterility and death — no doubt partly through the connection with winter, but also because of the whiteness
of the empty page, the 'paper that its whiteness de-
fends.' It might be said that he struggled all his life
against this 'whiteness,' which represents the special
enemy of writers. But it is also his own sterility, an
inability to live or act. Yet on the other hand it is a
curious mode of perfection, the class of unrealised
possibilities, and the place where all is dissolved. The
dramatic struggle of Mallarmé's life was to have worked
against the 'whiteness' which, at heart, he preferred to
the poem. For he was sure of its triumph, ironically sure

of the vanity of everything, 'The poem ends, whiteness returns'; thus death returns after the individual life, words and gestures vanish. And nothing proves that Being is better than Not-Being; each has its charm. That is why Mallarmé is the poet who above all others is occupied with how an existence — object, flower, effort, thought — disappears into nothing.[25] *The Swan* is an account of one of these disappearances; the bird, at first agitated by a wild hope, by cries and movements, for the air, when he sees that whiteness is stronger than he, resigns himself to renunciation. Whether we call the bird Life, Youth, Thought, Poetry, Movement, Action, makes little difference. What is important in the poem is the final victory of whiteness, the final immobility; an effect that no other poet has equalled.

[25] Or rather into Otherness. For Mallarmé, nothing was (as he explains in 'Music and Literature') an Otherness in relation to some existant. See also the Introduction, where I have tried to show how, for Mallarmé, Absence is a mode of Being, a rarefied and changed 'double' of Presence. This point is of importance because it shows the common origin of Mallarmé's preoccupation with whiteness, emptiness, silence, sterility, et cetera, and his taste for metaphor, relation and transitions between one object and another. The transition from reality to nothing is only the widest possible metaphor. But all metaphors demand a relation of similarity between their terms; in Mallarmé's work this relation is commonly the sensation of absence. In *The Swan* the similarity of winter and bird is their common whiteness. The winter only covers and absorbs the bird by means of this whiteness. I come back again to the idea suggested above:

'Fantom that to this place his brightness assigns.'

VICTORIOUSLY FLED

The poet, contemplating the splendours of a sunset, has had the half-humorous idea of effecting a suicide arranged with high romantic effect in the folds of this purple splendour. But at once he recalls himself, and back in his home he indulges in the fancy that the sky, deceived about his intentions, continues perhaps to expend in vain all its pomp, and prepares to drape magnificently a tomb which does not exist because the suicide did not take place.

And now night comes. Of all that splendour nothing remains, except in the room the blond tresses of a woman, the only gold which seems to remain over from the sunset. The 'puerile triumph' of the sunset has vanished almost entirely. What remains is in the woman's hair. She, lying naked on the cushions, suggests to the poet a golden imperial helmet whence pours a stream of roses.

HER PURE NAILS VERY HIGH DEDICATING THEIR ONYX

In this Sonnet, whose effect depends very largely on the actual sounds of the French words, Mallarmé seems to have made a wager to accomplish the impossible by choosing rhymes of the utmost difficulty — rhymes in 'yx' and 'ore' in the quatrains, inverted to 'ixe' and 'or' in the sestet. If one considers also the interior assonances with which Mallarmé enamelled his verse one must admit that the logical significance is likely to have suffered. The words themselves, rare and chiselled, suffice to give the poem the air of a jewel in gold and agate. Even without understanding the sense its beauty is apparent. A simple sequence of words like 'lampadophore,' 'onyx,' 'vespéral,' 'Phénix,' 'cinéraire amphore,' etc., count not merely by their sonority, but also by a sort of spiritual affinity which unites them. These words put side by side and connected alike by their significance and by the reflected sonorities ('L'Angoisse,' demanding 'lampadophore' — 'au Nord,' 'un or,' 'décor,' 'licornes') at once give the poem a unity of texture like that of a stiff brocade.

But the spirit demands a sense in what it reads; and not, as certain modern poets would have us believe, merely from a prosaic and vulgar preoccupation, but because the spirit lives by finding relations and finds its delight therein, so that to deprive one's phrases of sense is to renounce the richest system of relations that language has created. Mallarmé never neglected such opportunities. He refuses no means of interrelating the words of his poem, on the contrary he combines them all and complicates them, adding to the ties of primary significance a whole network of harmonic suggestions and interweaving the analogies of sound with the analogies of sense. But to a certain extent all these systems must interfere with one another. To choose beforehand, as Mallarmé has done here, such rare words, inevitably forces the curve of the thought to pass through certain predetermined points. Instead of proceeding in a straight line, as in prose, the thought traces an arabesque which may seem somewhat bizarre and extravagant. This is particularly the case here.

The subject is, I think, one of those poetic vigils, which caused Mallarmé such pain and anxiety because he wrote with difficulty, obeying 'the hard law'

> 'Of digging each night a new grave
> In the niggard cold earth of his brain.'

1st Quatrain. In his study, which his laborious anxiety keeps illumined, a lamp burns without producing ashes. Just so, one after another the poet's dreams are burned by a fire for ever renewed ('Phénix') without anything being left over to be gathered up in poems as in a 'cinerary urn.'

2nd Quatrain. No poems — no rhymes; for such I believe is the sense of this curious 'ptyx,' which exists in no dictionary and which Mallarmé seems to have forged. He took it from the Greek word πτύξ, which means a fold, the rhyme being the place where the verse folds back. But 'ptyx,' a word almost entirely without sense, yet capable of such rich rhyme, represents, I think, 'Rhyme for Rhyme's sake' — for the pleasure of the ear, 'abolished bibelot of sounding inanity.' This is, of course, a symbolic sense, but Mallarmé, who makes persistent comparison with the furniture of the room, may have been here thinking of those shells which ornamented many French nineteenth-century drawing rooms.

1st Tercet. Does nothing certain remain then from this vigil? Seeking as so often a poetical significance in his surroundings Mallarmé notices near the northward window a gleam of gold. As we fancy monsters in a fire, his eye finds a mythological scene of unicorns kicking up sparks at a nixie.

2nd Tercet. The poet then turns to see the window and the gleam of gold reflected in a mirror. He sees there the nixie, by now lying naked and dead, but he sees also the scintillation of the seven stars of the Great Bear ('of scintillations at once the septet'). All then does not perish. In this 'empty frame of oblivion' (which is Mallarméan for a mirror) something appears and remains: the stars of course, but also the poem itself henceforth motionless.

The idea that a scintillation of stars or of a poem is perhaps all that remains of an event occurs again in *Un Coup de Dés*:

RIEN N'AURA EU LIEU
                    EXCEPTÉ
                    PEUT-ÊTRE
                            UNE CONSTELLATION.

(Nothing will have taken place, except, perhaps, a constellation.)

THE MASS OF HAIR A FLAME'S FLIGHT TO THE EXTREME

The reader to whom the prose of *Divagations* is familiar will hardly fail to give this sonnet a smile of recognition. It is in fact taken from the *Declaration at a Fair*, the most fantastic of the anecdotes imagined by the poet. Of this I will give a brief summary.

Mallarmé, out walking with a young woman, unexpectedly finds himself in a suburban fair.[26] Amid the noise and glare of the central alleyway a stall attracts the attention of the pair; it is empty and bare. The old man, its owner, has indeed hung up as a curtain the cover of a mattress, which seems to hide something; in fact there is nothing to show. At this moment, a bizarre idea enters the head of the young woman. She orders the drum to be beaten; the crowd, to the patter of her companion, draws round, pays — a penny — and enters. The show offered them is simply the poet's mistress herself, standing on a table, fashionably dressed (in heliotrope), a flower-decorated hat on her fair hair. Before the general stupor Mallarmé feels the need to proclaim

[26] The Paris suburbs are industrial and proletarian in many places; without remembering this fact the English reader may misunderstand the anecdote. — Translator's note.

240

something — it hardly matters what, his meditations will do. He speaks the poem here translated, and then concludes with some phrases as well-intentioned as they are obscure. The crowd goes off, dumbfounded but good-tempered, and the couple resume their walk.

I am not here concerned with the sense of the anecdote itself. Mallarmé no doubt saw in it the meeting of Beauty and the Crowd. The only point that concerns us is this: Beauty is here represented by a woman, not a symbolic goddess but a real person, a 'contemporary of our evenings,' dressed, and, above all, with her hair done according to the taste of the period. It must be said in passing that the heliotrope dress, the flower-covered hat, and the braided hair represented, in Mallarmé's eyes, the *best* taste of the period, and our opinion in the matter — though it may give the anecdote an unforeseen atmosphere — has nothing to do with the case.

To return to the matter in hand, men have not, in most cases, a purely esthetic attitude towards the 'contemporaries of their evenings.' Mallarmé knows this very well when he describes a young soldier imagining himself slipping off his white gloves in 'the estimation of a high-placed garter.' [27] And his own imaginations — since he also is a man — though they may start from a less ingenuous foundation, are at bottom similar. The

[27] 'L'estimation d'une jarretière hautaine' — the play on the word *hautaine* is almost untranslatable, like too many slightly improper puns. — Translator's note.

fundamental attitude towards a woman is desire. But another problem preoccupies him; how to pass from desire to pure contemplation, how to 'sublimate' eroticism into beauty. I have tried in the Introduction to indicate the importance of this problem, which we here again find before us.

The Faun 'evaporated' the curves of women's naked bodies into 'an empty, sonorous, monotonous line.' But the Faun lived in a pagan world where nymphs go naked. In the modern, clothed world, sensuality attaches itself to partial nudities. That of the hair, above all, haunted Mallarmé. One can retrace the development sketched in the Introduction simply by examining the poet's successive impressions before women's hair. In *Apparition* it evokes the nostalgia of childhood:

'And I thought I saw the Fairy with her cap of Brightness.'

In *Anguish* the sad negation of a bestial love:

'nor hollow
In your tresses' impurity a dismal storm.'

In *Herodias*, a sterile and metallic purity:

'my hairs, which are not flowers
To spread forgetfulness of human ills,
But gold, for ever virgin of aromatics,
In their cruel lights and matt palenesses
To observe the sterile coldness of metal,

. . . . .

Metals which give my youthful tresses
A fatal splendour and their massive sway!'

Most curiously, in the *Faune* this hardness is dissolved:

'And the splendid bath of their hair disappears
In the shimmer and shuddering, oh diamonds!'

The hair later becomes the violently erotic, 'dishevelled tuft' which joins with the 'considerable tuft' of one of the last sonnets. From this point, the creative imagination of the poet takes up its work. Above all, he is fascinated by two metaphors. First, there is the analogy of golden hair and the sunset, which indeed forms the subject of the sonnet *Victoriously fled*. Second, there is the hair spread like a silk flag ('What silk embalmed'). The two images, flame and flag, are here united in that of a torch, seen in the imagination as a standing woman with flowing hair.

Let us now take the sonnet line by line.[28]

'The mass of hair, a flame's flight'

gives the essential idea of a torch.

'to the extreme
Occident of desires there to unfold all'

[28] In the quotations I have re-established the punctuation, not given in the text; consequently it must, like the interpretation, be taken as only hypothetical.

means 'made (primitively) to be unrolled to the extreme
west of desires.' This is the natural movement of the
amatory instinct, the immediate erotic use. 'Extreme
west' comes from the association with the sunset, the
idea of a flame being readily confused with that of
desire. Art, on the contrary, a deviation from the primitive instinct, means repressing the inclination, the spontaneous movement, and rejecting the energy towards
its source, the flame towards the east:

> 'Settles'

— This is the esthetic mode of action —

> '(call it the dying of a diadem)'

— forms, in dying, a diadem —

> 'Towards the crowned brow its ancient hearth.'

Art is this plaited wreath of hair which denies itself
to sensual love.

But this will involve a certain disappointment. What,
no more gold, no more flame?

> 'But, deprived of gold, to sigh.'

The consolation that is sighed for is

> 'This live cloud'

— the hair, obviously —

> 'The ignition of a fire always internal'

— the flame, though forced back, is always there —

'Originally the only one'

— since there is only one flame, one vital energy —

'should continue
In the jewel of the eye, serious or mocking.'

Something remains naked; the eyes, which do not lie, but frankly and laughingly admit the sensual origins of art.

'A nakedness of a tender hero'

is that of the eye:

'. . . defames
That which . . .'

'Defames' is the hardest word of the sonnet; it is to be taken in its etymological sense, 'divulges,' 'reveals to the crowd' the secret nakedness of that which, Woman or Beauty,

'nor moving star nor fire on the finger'

i.e. without extraneous ornament ('fire' recalls the only veritable jewel, the eye, and prepares for the 'rubies' of the last lines):

'Nought but simplifying the woman with glory
Accomplishes by its head, flaming, the exploit

Of sowing with rubies the doubt it has grazed
As might a joyous and tutelary torch.'

That is to say, wakes, in the obscurities of the soul, a doubt (that which also embarrasses the audience at the fair: 'What is the good of this desirable, but intangible woman? What is the good of Beauty?'), irritates this doubt, 'grazes' it, yet draws from it a certain splendour, exactly as the light of a torch 'grazing' the dark, none the less scatters it with rubies.

THE TOMB OF EDGAR POE

This piece needs rather a literary commentary than an explanation. It contains two or three of Mallarmé's best-known lines:

'Such as to himself eternity's changed him'

might serve as the theme for a dissertation on Death and the Absolute in the poet's works, while

'Giving a sense more pure to the words of their tribe'

might serve as epigraph to a Mallarméan esthetic.

'This sonnet,' writes Mallarmé, 'was recited at the unveiling, at Baltimore, of a block of basalt as a monument to Poe, with which America weighted down the poet's light shadow, *in order to make sure that it never reappeared.*' The ironical remark that is here italicised is a trace of the indignation that animates the whole sonnet.

The two quatrains appear to sketch the bas-reliefs whose absence from the monument the poet regrets in the first tercet. Eternity presents the poet under his true shape, as the angel of death; the age which misunderstood him is the 'Hydra's vile spasm.' The strangeness of the poet's voice (really an attempt at poetic purity) the vulgar take to be the effect of drink. The world, from earth to sky, shows itself hostile to genius. This hostility should form the subject of the bas-reliefs. If not, we can at least make this block a boundary stone against future stupidity.

There are few obscurities. 'They' is an intentionally contemptuous reference to the members of the amorphous crowd, which divides into individuals for an instant, only to reunite with 'a Hydra's vile spasm.' 'The dishonoured flow of some dark brew' may, in view of Mallarmé's more than metaphysical poetic habits, mean stout.

It seems harder to explain clearly:

'Calm block fallen down here from some dark disaster.'

It may be an allusion to the volcanic origin of basalt. At any rate, this idea of a cosmic catastrophe makes even stranger the notion of this immense, bare block, an erratic rock or giant meteorite. At first apparently meaningless, it rises black, calm and strange, like Poe himself, 'Such as to himself eternity's changed him.' This is why we are not astonished at the irrelevance;

the overtones of rock and poet are too strongly related. The 'dark disaster' whence the block has fallen is subtly confused with the disasters of genius, the struggle of angel and hydra grows more cosmic, and Poe, if possible, more granitic. Thus the last tercet suddenly acquires a terrifying and desolate grandeur. For this idea of an erratic block suggests an immense, empty plain, from which all life has disappeared. (Notice how, in the first tercet, all idea of human beings has disappeared, and there is no longer question of any but elemental forces — rock and cloud.) The spectacle presented to the imagination is that of an empty earth and an atmosphere of desolation. The last line can now display its sinister extent. At the end of the sonnet 'Blasphemy,' like a flock of crows, wheels in an empty sky unable to cross a black boundary, over which the wrath of God seems to hang.

THE TOMB OF CHARLES BAUDELAIRE

The antithesis here expressed is that which suggested the title itself of Baudelaire's *Fleurs du Mal* — 'Unhealthy Flowers,' Gautier writes in his preface, 'such as grow in the black mud in which the paving stones of a great town are set.' 'Fleurs du Ruisseau' (flowers of the gutter) is also a common expression. It is not surprising then that Mallarmé, wishing to celebrate Baudelaire, should have remembered a scene which the latter had sung in one of his most famous poems *Le Vin des Chiffoniers.*

> 'Souvent à la clarté rouge d'un réverbère
> Dont le vent bat la flamme et tourmente le verre,
> Au cœur d'un vieux faubourg, labyrinthe fangeux.' [29]

And the same mud and flame form the material of Mallarmé's poem.

1st *Quatrain.* 'Le temple enseveli' is the drain. Some English readers may not be sufficiently familiar with Paris to understand at once 'la bouche sépulcrale d'égout.' 'Bouche d'égout' is the technical word to express those vertical openings cut in the thickness of the pavement down which the surface drainage disappears. It therefore presents almost exactly the appearance of the entrance to a tomb.

As so frequently Mallarmé delights to use the most trivial terms. Here we have 'Bouche d'égout,' elsewhere 'mouchoir,' 'ne pas fermer l'œil,' 'détaler,' 'les absolus lieux' (for a W.C.). It is one of the chief characteristics of his poetical method to take as a point of departure, however far and however high be his aim, the most familiar and the most concrete facts or expressions.

'Slobbering mud and rubies' gives the antithesis —

[29] *The Wine of the Ragpickers:*

Often in the red light of a street lamp
When the wind blows the flame and beats at the glass,
In the muddy labyrinth of an old slum.

mud, flame. 'Rubis' expressing probably the reflections of the street lamp in the gutter:

> 'Abominably some idol of Anubis
> All its muzzle aflame with wild barking.'

The 'bouche d'égout' with its sepulchral air is also the door of the temple imagined to exist in the depths behind, reminiscent naturally of Egyptian buried temples — hence its wide opened mouth suggests the barking muzzle of the dog-headed God. 'Flambé' is related to 'rubis': they both derive from 'the red light of a street lamp.' 'Divulge' means 'reveal to everyone.'

2nd *Quatrain*. 'Ou' [30] indicates the beginning of a new image with the same meaning. The poet now sees the street lamp above the drain. Since the lamp has a wick, it is an oil lamp. 'Le gaz récent' is the nascent gas which escapes from the oil and twists the wick in burning it. Symbolically the flame represents the poetry of Baudelaire born of the squalor of the life of the flesh. 'Essuyeuse on le sait des opprobres subis': the dirt of the wick corresponds to the miseries of Baudelaire's life; 'Essuyeuse' is used in the sense of 'essuyer une tempête.' 'Il' (the gas) lights (produces as it burns) an immortal pubis. The 'pubis' is the triangular and dishevelled flame, 'Dont le vol selon le réverbère découche.' The lamp is a hanging one and sways in the

[30] Cf. for the same use of *ou*, *To the overwhelming blackness husht* — 'or was it' — and the French text of the *Faune*, line 10: 'ou si les femmes.'

wind, but whatever angle it takes the flame mounts up straight. Thus relatively to the lamp the flight of the flame is often a deviation from its proper course, as the pejorative word 'découche' suggests.

Similarly Baudelaire's poetry appears to be a deviation from normal standards but is, Mallarmé declares, in reality an upward flight.

Sestet. This refers to the monument which it was proposed to erect to Baudelaire, with funds raised from the *Book of Homage*, for which this sonnet was written (Bibliography of 1898).

The sense is, I think, as follows: What votive wreath, with its dried-up leaves, could equal, on this monument, the atmosphere of a great city at night, with its play of light and shade (the subject of the quatrains), and which Mallarmé identifies with Baudelaire's spirit (celle son Ombre même) morbid, poisonous and none the less one of our poetic resources.

The construction of this part is very elliptic. It should be taken thus:

'Quel feuillage seché dans les cités sans soir, votif pourra bénir comme elle (pourra) se rasseoir [31] contre le marbre, vainement, de Baudelaire, Au voile qui la ceint absente avec frissons,[32] Celle, son

[31] *I.e.* What foliage, etc., could have, by its benedictory action, as great efficacy as his shade if it were to return to sit . . .

[32] *Absente* and *vainement* correspond to the same idea. Since the spirit of Baudelaire is in Mallarmé's mind identified with the

Ombre même (un poison tutélaire), qui est toujours à respirer si nous en périssons.'

TOMB [of Verlaine]

This *Tomb* [of *Verlaine*] being one of the most obscure
of the poems, any detailed explanation will seem at
first sight extremely dubious. Accordingly, I wish for
once to change my method, and instead of immediately
presenting the reader with what seems to me the most
plausible explanation, I will ask him to follow the
actual course of my thought. I set out from the idea
that in a poem by Mallarmé all the words are necessarily
related, either by the plain sense or by relations of
overtones; to explain the poem is the same thing as to
make apparent this system of relations. Such a point of
departure would be mistaken in discussing any other
poet, even the greatest, even a genius like Shakespeare,
for though Shakespeare surpasses Mallarmé infinitely
in many respects, he was perfectly capable of putting
two metaphors side by side without the least relation
between them; Mallarmé could not have done so; this
is an experimental fact. This coherence of the poem
is my only guiding principle: if I give a false explanation

_____

nocturnal atmosphere of Paris, his spirit can come to sit on his
monument without any one distinguishing it from the atmosphere
which is actually there.

Frissons is the shimmering of the street lamps.

it is, I am sure, because the true one, of which I am ignorant, offers even greater coherence, more 'reflections' between words, more echoes between the different parts of the poem.

The sense of the tercets, here fairly clear, will serve as a clue. What do they mean? Verlaine, hidden in the grass, is undergoing a new experience. He is looking at death, this rivulet, from close to. And he learns that it has been calumniated, that its waters are neither so deep nor so terrible as they are commonly said to be. It is the naive belief of a vagabond who has always lived close to nature, and whose ingenuousness, once more, has saved him from too 'sombre beliefs.' And, as a matter of fact, who has rendered death so frightful, has 'calumniated' it? The Christian religion. And the historical fact that Verlaine did struggle all his life between his pagan and his Catholic tendencies indicates that we are on the right track. Moreover, the question of religion is one of Mallarmé's themes, as can be seen in his *Medallion* of Verlaine (in *Divagations*) where he insists on the poet's sincerity, his courageous readiness to become a subject of scandal, and his natural shamelessness. Verlaine, for Mallarmé, was a man who had been naively ready to admit, when his mind was not darkened by religious beliefs, the nakedness of his sins, and to admit it with a 'terrible probity.' And now, after his death, he learns how empty were the menaces of punishment with which he was overwhelmed by religion, whereas his ingenuous love of nature was right.

Provided with this clue, let us now consider the quatrains. At first sight it is impossible to know exactly what is this rock which the blast rolls, and which will not be stopped even by the 'hands' which seek 'the likeness to all human ills.' But I notice certain spontaneous associations: 'black' suggests the 'sombre beliefs' spoken of above; 'pious' clearly belongs to a religious context; and the ominous 'mould of human ills' seems to be vaguely connected with the general idea of original sin.

The second quatrain is more revealing. The cooing dove has an air of paganism. But above all

> 'the future's ripened star
> Whose glittering will silver o'er the crowd' [33]

agrees with the eventual appearance of a riper wisdom, a more luminous doctrine enlightening humanity. This future light is to-day hidden by the clouds, which oppress the star with nubile folds — that is to say, which *'obnubilate'* it, since little by little the evidence makes it clear that 'nubile' has nothing to do with marriage, and is simply derived from *nubes*.

Hence arises a possible explanation of the second quatrain. Here and now, on the earth, though we are not without paganism, though poets like Verlaine can sing ingenuously, yet our sky is always hidden by sombre

[33] Cf. 'Silenced to the overwhelming cloud.'

beliefs. These, nevertheless, will be blown away like clouds from before the natural sun that will be enjoyed by man in the future.

Immediately the first line becomes clear. The black rock is this very cloud of religious beliefs and the idea of sin. Mallarmé has elsewhere compared rocks to massive and sombre clouds; he has spoken of the 'overwhelming cloud' made 'of lava and basalt.' [33] The image is therefore a possible one; moreover, a cloud is the only sort of rock the wind can roll.

This is the point at which to relate the two future verbs of the two quatrains 'will not be stayed' and 'will silver.' They are drawn from the same idea, express the same hope; 'the future's ripened star' will shine precisely because nothing will be able to check the flight of the clouds and oppressive thoughts. What is it meanwhile which tries to check them? First of all a spontaneous resistance, the clouds being 'angry that the wind rolls' them. And secondly, the pious hands of those who see in sin the only possible explanation and origin, the only 'mould' of human ills. I must admit that for a long time I found these pious hands fumbling at a cloud very strange; Mallarmé always takes as the starting point of his metaphors real sights, often very familiar ones. What sight was the origin of this? I think I have found a reply having at least some probability; the 'pious hands' are those of Christ, on a crucifix, extended in the sky. The sonnet, which is inscribed 'Anniversary — January

1897,' was almost certainly suggested by the sight of a cemetery. It seems easy enough to reconstitute, from this point, the real images which served as material for the poem; the low and heavy sky, the clouds almost as solid as the tombs beneath, the lifted arms of the crucifix appearing to touch the clouds, and in spite of this a dove, the hope of the 'ripened' sun, grass, and the murmur of the streamlet. From this collection of objects Mallarmé composed his poem. The clouds became the sombre beliefs, and also perhaps the fatal destiny of Verlaine, all the miseries of his life. But what must triumph in the end is that pagan wisdom known also to the poet. For that matter, the vicissitudes of life are over for him; whoever follows the course of this life (this 'leap till now external') sees it finish in the peaceful contemplation of death, a calumniated stream. Verlaine, once a vagabond, now a peaceable faun, buried in the grass, watching a trickle of water of which he has no longer the least fear, does not even drink from it, does not even cut short his breath, since he now enjoys a poetic immortality; he remains content to surprise death as an amused observer, naively in accord with nature.

HOMMAGE [à Wagner]

It is very hard to write a commentary on this poem without producing an unwieldly résumé of Mallarmé's

theory of the theatre: (*Drame, Danse, Opéra et Ode*).
I refer the reader to those pages, many of them brilliantly written, which are headed 'Crayonné au Théâtre' and will be found in *Divagations*, also to the essay devoted to Wagner — *Richard Wagner, rêverie d'un poète français* — and to various passages here and there which deal with religious ceremonies.

A familiarity with these writings justifies a difficult interpretation. Mallarmé's attitude to the Wagnerian theatre was two-sided. He hailed the efforts of a genius who rescued the theatre from its realistic fallacies — unchanging *décor* and realistic characters. On the other hand, Mallarmé was convinced that Wagner was wrong in trying to make a true theatre by what was more or less an attempt to unite Shakespeare with Beethoven, music with drama.[34] He disliked the Legend and dreamed of a more abstract theatre, a kind of religious ceremony — an ideal performance using music, poetry and the dance — in the sense in which the Mass is a performance of the divine drama. I am afraid of misrepresenting a very exalted speculation by any further description. Wagner — the musician — has done — not quite successfully — that which books did before it was attempted by the theatre; the old realistic theatre is dead. Such are the ideas of the sonnet.

Roughly speaking, the first quatrain deals with the decay of the realistic drama. But, on closer examination,

[34] *Letter to Vittorio Pici* quoted by Thibaudet.

it must be admitted that such expressions as: 'tassement du principal pilier,' 'moire,' and 'manque de mémoire' remain mysterious. One may find explanations but they are very dubious. The only related text that I know is to be found in *Divagations*: 'Maintenant que suprêmement on ouït craquer jusque dans sa membrure définitive la menuiserie et le cartonnage de la bête . . .' For my part I imagine, listening to the first lines, the curtain — a funeral pall in its way — falling before the stage and its scenery. The 'principal pilier' being the drama in its present fallen state. The entire realistic set is done for.

The second quatrain is easier: 'let us stop trying to drag books onto the stage; let us thrust the old triumphant revelry ('vieil ébat triomphal') into a cupboard. Lines 6 and 7 are made less obscure if they are compared with the quatrain written for a library.

> 'Ci gît le noble vol humain
> Cendre ployée avec les livres
> Pour que toute tu la délivres
> Il faut en prendre un dans ta main.'

'Millier' (line 6) means multitude.

In the tercets we have the new theatre. Richard Wagner the God, hated by the 'souriant fracas originel,' that is to say, the incoherent noises of the auditorium — the multitudinous chaos — throws out rays of transcendent light (they are identified with the upward flight of stairs) and among them there are those which lead to the courts of the new temple imagined by Mallarmé.

'Trompettes tout haut d'or pâmé sur les vélins' is in apposition. Wagner is the founder; he performs a brilliant act of consecration upon the stage, the consecration of the idea, that idea which was apparent in the gold of the illumination, but might be discerned in the ink of the manuscript, half visible for all its blackness. 'Mal tu par l'encre même.'

HOMMAGE (*à Puvis de Chavannes*)

This hommage to Puvis de Chavannes is perfectly symmetrical in its construction; it is very much easier to understand than the preceding poem.

The first two quatrains are made from a single sentence. 'Always at sunrise a herdsman walks towards a spring' ('Toute Aurore a son pâtre marchant vers la source'). The tercets are composed of another sentence: 'Thus you saw ahead, you saw far enough to bring the age to a new spring ('Ainsi tu vis par avance, tu vis de conduire le temps à la source nouvelle').

'. . . gourde — A crisper' — the fingers numb with clutching . . . the herdsman's stick beating a pace ahead of his step ('Le long de son pas futur') is an admirable image, not only because it is concise, but because of its relation to the poem as a whole. Everything is 'in advance'; the sunrise is in advance of the day, the herdsman is in advance of the living and Puvis is in advance of his times. Thus the stick strikes the future, there where he will set foot, where the spring will gush forth. The key to the relationship is a tense — and this is in fact the meaning of the *hommage*.

ALL THE SOUL INDRAWN

This is advice to a beginner, an 'art of poetry' in a lighter tone. What is poetry? A puff of smoke, into which the soul is entirely withdrawn. Line follows line, verse verse, each element dissolving, 'abolished' in the following element:

> 'All the soul indrawn
> When slowly we exhale it
> In many rounds of smoke
> Lost in other rounds'

And, of course, there is no smoke without fire — nor ashes. Poetry presupposes, beyond itself, the actual life of the poet. In the same way the smoke proves, somewhere, the existence of a lighted cigar. Moreover, if the smoke is to rise in clear blue rings, it must burn carefully. Wherein lies this science? In a certain slowness, to begin with:

> 'When *slowly* we exhale it'

but above all in the extreme delicacy with which, at the

point where it burns, the reduction must take place, the smoke escaping and the ash remaining.

The metaphor is drawn from familiar objects, the tone is joking: hence the irony of the succeeding verses:

> 'So the choir of songs
> Flies it to your lip'

But the advice is serious: 'Exclude, from poetry, the ash of the real, — that is to say, in practice, avoid words with too precise a sense which will erase, with a stroke of the pen, 'your vague literature.' I have already shown, in the Introduction, how closely this is related to Verlaine's *Art of Poetry*. The latter's exhortation:

> 'Music before all things'

becomes

> 'Smoke before all things,'

but the technical advice remains all the same.

> 'Il faut aussi que tu n'ailles point
> Choisir les mots sans quelque méprise:
> Rien de plus cher que la chanson grise
> Où l'Indécis au Précis se joint.' [35]
> (*Art Poétique — Jadis et Naguère.*)

It seems to me interesting, moreover, to put beside this poem a phrase from *Divagations*:

[35] Also you must never go
To choose words without some mistake:
Nothing so dear as the grey song
Where the precise and vague are joined.

261

'I unite this meditation with the smoke (of my cigar) so as to be able to follow them both, satisfied, diminishing together, before sitting down to a poem, where it will reappear, perhaps, veiled. . . .'

TO THE SOLE CARE OF VOYAGING

To whom is this piece and the toast it proposes addressed? It does not greatly matter. But in general it is addressed to the artist who, like Mallarmé himself, claims to go beyond the too facile 'Indies,' the too easy exploitation of riches 'splendid' but 'troubled,' and to set out for a purer end, if such exist. For the end of this traveller may perhaps be to round all the capes, for the pleasure of rounding them, to fly to the limits of the sensible world, through increasing absences, towards the realm of silence and whiteness, thus establishing a liaison or metaphor between that which is and that which is not.

One can understand this poem best by comparing it with two others: *Salutation*, which is the first poem of the volume, and the sonnet of *The Swan*.[36] There is here the same air of the sea as in *Salutation:*

'Our sail's white solicitude,'

being here made explicit as:

[36] See page 102.

> '. . . the sole care of voyaging
> Beyond a splendid troubled Ind.'

All the same there is this evident difference: what was
in the former poem only the half-humorous enthusiasm
of a banquet, with its evocation of sirens turning somer-
saults, and of happy cruising, has become here an inflexible and 'pale' determination. The sonnet of *The
Swan* supplies us with more profound analogies. In
both we have to do with a passage between movement
and immobility, with an effort which dies down, a cry
which expires. In *The Swan* the immobile term of
comparison is the winter landscape; the revolt of the
bird which seems in the first lines about to break the
constraint, little by little grows weaker and is stilled.
Here the immobile term is the determination of 'pale
Vasco' who, for nothing in the world, will 'veer his
helm,' and naturally the immobility triumphs in the
last words of the sonnet, just before the arrival, thus
prepared, of silence. Against this inflexible will there
break (the term of movement like the vain hope of the
swan) the calls of life, of the earth, of 'the cape that
his poop is rounding.' There are treasures, though
desperately 'useless' ones, and fabulous veins and lodes
of ore buried, as in *Hérodias:*

> 'Under the sombre sleep of a primaeval soil.'

A bird, messenger of these treasures, announcing the

splendours waiting to be seized, has come to perch on a spar of the ship and thence, amid the spurting foam, monotonously cries his message and repeats his call. In vain! The poop has already turned the cape, the helm has not veered an inch; the earth withdraws and is lost — 'night, despair and adamant.'

The bird's cry which was already, as it were, an echo of the sleeping treasures, provokes in its turn only an echo of that echo, still paler and more fugitive, the last ricochet of the real before the final silence, the smile on the traveller's face.

Thus the poem tells of the vanishing of a cry, as *The Swan* was the extinction of an effort.

The syntax of the French is dislocated to follow the movement of the thought. It may be reconstructed thus (words occurring in the text are italicised):

(Que) *ce salut* — (salut) *au seul souci de voyager outre une Inde splendide et trouble — soit* (pour toi) *le messager* (venu) *du temps* (in the semi-religious sense of the word 'secular' or 'temporal': the real, as opposed to the spiritual life; the more ordinary idea of the artist doubling the cape of time, assuring himself an immortality, is not excluded) *comme* (a messenger of that world to Vasco) *toujours un oiseau d'annonce nouvelle écumait en ébats* (*i.e.* hovered, a flake of foam) *sur quelque vergue plongeante bas avec la caravelle* — (oiseau) *qui criait* (the transitive verb, announced) *monotonement, sans que la barre ne varie, un inutile gise-*

264

ment — Nuit, désespoir et pierrerie — par son chant reflété [37] *jusqu'au sourire du pâle Vasco.*

DOES ALL PRIDE SMOKE OUT EVENING

This piece forms, with the two following ones numbered II and III by Mallarmé himself, a kind of triptych of still lives. The subject of each is taken from furniture, perhaps from the same room. Their relative obscurity comes from the fact that the poet makes use of allusions, doubtless quite evident to him, to objects which he saw, but of which we have to guess the nature.

The point of departure for this first poem is a console, gilded no doubt, supporting a heavy slab of marble. I have often wondered whether the room might not perhaps be that of Villiers de l'Isle-Adam, of whom Mallarmé gives such a beautiful portrait in *Divagations*. Perhaps it is the 'historical' room of some fallen prince. In any case it is that of a man once powerful, now abandoned, the heir of 'many a rich fallen trophy.' It would not be surprising though if these trophies were in fact purely spiritual. But however this may be, one fact is evident. The room is without a fire. From this springs the essential idea of the poem. On the one hand the empty grate, on the other the console, the only object in the room which resembles a glowing fireplace and

[37] *Reflété* refers to *gisement*; the smile is the last reflection of the ore, by the intermediary of the song.

chimney-piece, a glitter of gold beneath the marble, but a glitter which is ironical and icy.

The sense of the first quatrain is simply: Must then all glory perish? The pride of glory is compared to a torch that a shake, some day, puts out fatally. Its jet of flame — tufted, blown about by the wind, burning, ephemeral [38] — (I note here a few harmonies of the French word *bouffée*) cannot survive the inevitable end. Then from the torch there mounts only a black smoke, the night of the past, which envelops everything, like the darkness after sunset. Whence the expression *fume du soir* ('smoke out evening') where *soir* ('evening') is a direct complement.

The rest of the sonnet presents no great difficulties. I imagine that the carving of the gilt console might represent or suggest some monster with claws ('Clutching as though with claws') — the claws also being comparable to flames — crushed under the weight of the marble, chimney mantel and sepulchral slab at the same time. At least such an idea falls in with the notion of a last effort against a fatal decay. Over against the empty mantel-piece the console glitters and writhes in a supreme protest, but in vain. In the final tercet —

> 'Under the heavy marble
> It enisles no fire is lit
> But the glittering console.'

[38] *Immortelle bouffée* seems to be an ironical allusion to the cliché *gloire immortelle*.

the word 'enisles' is perhaps a little surprising, but it seems to be explicable and to merit consideration. Without the glittering console and its poetic significance the slab might pass unnoticed, would remain one among many objects. Physically the console lifts the slab up, holds it in the air and brings it into notice — isolates it. Morally it offers it to our contemplation, exacting from us, by this mute interjection, some finer interpretation. Just as some painters are persuaded that no matter what group of objects, if one looks at it long enough, may become the subject of a picture, unfold a plastic idea, so Mallarmé believed that any spectacle can, under the poet's eye, become a 'sign,' that is to say, the subject of a poem. For instance in the *Divagations*, writing of the bear of the *Spectacle interrompu*; and again the dancer in *Ballets*: 'The only exercise of the imagination consists . . . in patiently and passively enquiring before each step, before each attitude, before these spots or patches, elongated or balloon-shaped "What does this mean?", or, better still, to read it by inspiration . . . then, by a communication of which her smile seems to reveal the secret, without delay she yields you, through the final veil which always remains, the nudity of your concept and silently writes your vision in the form of a "sign," which she is.' On this point see also the Introduction, and the gloss of *Toast Funèbre* with regard to the flowers seen by the poet which:

'. . . rain and diamonds, his diaphanous look
Remaining there on the flowers of which none fades,
Isolates in the hour and the day's luminosity!'

The meaning of 'isolates' is evident here: it is the bringing into evidence of the object for a poetic transmutation. In the sonnet we are considering this interpretation is then: The marble slab evokes on the one hand the chimney-piece of the empty fireplace, on the other the sepulchral slab, a sign of the inevitability of decadence. Thus the 'marble' is closely knit up with the central idea of the poem. Considered 'under the light proper to the dream' it has taken on significance.

RISEN FROM THE SPRINGING CROUP

The theme of this poem is a glass vase which is empty. From this vase there ought to spring a rose. But there is none.

Most readers of Mallarmé take the words 'vase' and 'rose' in their literal sense. And it is quite possible they are right. But I think a more plausible hypothesis is that 'verrerie' is the glass of a chandelier — 'éphémère' suggests the elaboration of a Venetian chandelier — and the rose its light. I see two reasons for this, one that the poet has put his verses into the mouth of a mythological figure painted on the ceiling — 'Moi, sylphe de ce froid plafond,' and one imagines him more easily referring to some object near at hand, the other that the idea of the room being dark is constantly insisted on:

> 'The bitter vigil unflowered'

and

> 'A rose amid the darkness'

The sylph would like, no doubt, to see a rose of flame burst out in the darkness; but this room lacks light as well as fire; by a strange caprice the chandelier obstinately refuses to open out its flower of brightness, and this refusal is the subject of the poem.

The theme is given from the beginning. The neck of the glass-work stretches out, rising upwards, and then, just at the moment when the rose ought to emerge, the effort is interrupted. 'Forgotten' suggests that no one is interested in the drama, because the room is empty and dark. 'Forgotten' is clearly one of the words that connects this poem with the preceding one. Thus, in the obscurity, a tentative is broken off. A strange arrest, thinks the sylph, strange peculiarity of individual caprice. Even in their embrace, it seems, two lovers do not find on their united lips the same taste. There is no such thing as complete union. The lips of the glass-work, pressed against the night, ought to expand in a kiss, a rose of light. No, the vase is so pure, so emptied by some 'inexhaustible widowhood,' that it rejects this embrace. The kiss fails and dies.

The idea of purity, of religious abstention, occurs

often in Mallarmé, and that of joined lips forming a
burning flower is also familiar to him: *e.g.* in *Rondel II*:

> 'Si tu veux nous nous aimerons
> Avec tes lèvres sans le dire
> Cette rose ne l'interromps
>
> .   .   .   .   .
>
> 'Muet muet entre les ronds
> Sylphe dans la pourpre d'empire
> Un baiser flambant se déchire
> Jusqu'aux pointes des ailerons
> Si tu veux nous nous aimerons.' [39]

This latter use of 'sylph' suggests moreover this question; may it not be that the sylph of the sonnet is not
the painted figure but the kiss itself which did not occur,
the flame and rose? The 'lover' would then be the chandelier and the 'mother' the night.

Notes.—(This is a comment of Roger Fry's, writing
to C. Mauron. — J. B.):

1. I've put in my explanation of *éphémère*: don't you
agree? It's so exactly the word for one of those elaborate

[39] If you wish we will make love
With your lips saying nothing
That rose do not interrupt

.   .   .   .   .

Mute mute between the rounds
Sylph in the imperial purple
A flaming kiss tears itself
Right to the tips of the wings
If you wish we will make love.

blown-glass affairs with glass flowers (which by the by I suspect suggested the whole theme).

2. Apropos of the joined lips which the poet compares to a rose, I cannot forbear quoting also this quatrain from the 'Vers de circonstance':

Verre d'Eau
Ta lèvre contre le cristal
Gorgée à gorgée y compose
Le souvenir pourpre et vital
De la moins éphémère rose.

A Glass of Water

Your lip against the crystal
Sip by sip composes
The memory red and vital
Of least ephemeral roses.

A LACE CURTAIN STANDS EFFACED

The poet has turned towards the window. He sees its lace curtains slightly parted; and at once he thinks of the curtains of a bed. But these let us see, in the gap they leave, only, once more, an absence, and the paleness of the window pane.

This is the point of departure suggested in the first strophe. The reader may well ask what is the meaning of 'In doubt of the supreme Game.' That indeed is the point of greatest obscurity, and two hypotheses seem equally tenable. The 'supreme Game' may be the act of love. It would certainly not surprise one that Mallarmé should evoke here the fantastic embrace, so oddly pure and ethereal, of the two curtains: and then there would follow naturally enough —

> 'This unanimous white conflict
> Of a garland with its like.'

In this case 'A lace curtain stands effaced' would suggest some ecstatic faintness; 'the doubt of the supreme Game' would be to be at once two and one. At the end of the second quatrain 'burying' would seem only to allow of the interpretation, the burying of a seed, fecundation which, however, would not be accomplished since the 'conflict' is too pure and ethereal:

> 'Is floating more than burying.'

The sequence of ideas would be: None the less a birth might take place, that of a poet. Certainly this idea of birth which is insisted on at the end of the poem is the strongest support of this first hypothesis. The associations, bed — love-making — birth, make a strong and natural sequence. That in the poem the bed is absent, the embrace only of two curtains, and what gives birth a mandola, is no objection. Mallarmé, who when he wished could achieve the sharpest precision, here evidently remains purposely vague, musically vague, in harmony with the vaporous vision which is his point of departure. The words of this reverie, which suggest floating whiteness, are bound together more by their overtones than by their crude and literal meaning:

> 'Its too sharp sense will overscrawl
> Your vague literature.'

This dubious birth of a poet from the womb of a mandola

> 'Whose hollow void is musical'

and

> 'Towards some window pane,'

that is to say, towards evasion, coming after the equally uncertain coupling of the two lace curtains, does not seem to me too preposterous. Our everyday thought makes many astonishing leaps and relates objects by even more absurd associations. Why then should we be surprised at the antics of a chimaera?

None the less I find it hard to believe that Mallarmé really meant love-making by the words 'the supreme Game,' especially with a capital letter. For he habitually only speaks of Poetry with this emphasis. 'The transmutation, wherefor man exists,' he writes in *Divagations*, 'goes from the fact to the ideal.' This is precisely, for him, 'the supreme Game' which he is playing at the moment he contemplates the curtains. And this game consists in denying the reality in the foreground (and that is why it is essentially a 'doubt') in order to fix the mind only on the correspondences, the analogies, and the mysterious associations. It is in this way that the spirit succeeds in giving a sense to the world. The banal reality is destroyed, the mere curtains of the window disappear, dissolved by his reverie, denied, 'abolished' by 'the doubt of "the supreme Game."' By this spiritual metamorphosis they become something 'rare and strange' — the curtains of an absence of bed. Strange curtains indeed — those of a bed fall heavily, give the effect of drapery, of hiding, 'burying' — but these float, mount across the window as though escaping, airy whitenesses, towards the paleness of the sky, inviting us also to some evasion. Bed, window, whiteness, evasion — for any one who knows Mallarmé these words irresistibly evoke the idea of a poetic birth. They are indeed the same associations as in the *Don du Poëme* [40] :

'I bring you the child of an Idumaean night.'

There we find exactly the same window growing pale, the woman sleeping, the tenderness of maternity, and even that vague musical sweetness which recalls ancient instruments:

'And with your voice recalling viol and clavecin,
With your faded finger, will you press the breast

[40] See pages 58 and 186–7.

274

Whence flows in sibylline whiteness woman
For lips made hungry by the blue virgin air?'

For we must note that the sonnet *A lace curtain stands
effaced* appears to be a poem of dawn. It is the end of
the triptych. The first sonnet *Does all Pride smoke out
evening* has the atmosphere of twilight after sunset,
the torch put out, the spreading smoke, shadow and
solitude descending. The second is the middle of the
night — 'a rose in the darkness.' In the third the window is paling and the whole series is connected, by
many evocations, with the poet's own vigils, with their
cold solitude, their often sterile efforts:

'And the bitter vigil unflowered
The forgotten neck stops short,'

and finally to the dawn when the poem comes to birth.
Then Mallarmé goes to see his wife, a mother also. The
dawn for him always kept this flavour of paling windows
and maternity, at once musical and sad. In this view
then the poet in whose mind 'dreams are gilt' is the
essential figure of the sonnet, and hence 'the supreme
Game' must be his poetry rather than his love.

Let me note finally with what delicacy Mallarmé
escapes from the too crude idea of birth by the expression — in the French a strange enough one at first
sight — 'selon nul ventre que le sien.' 'De son ventre'
would be horrible. As it is, the idea remains but blurred,
and 'filial' with its suggestions of tenderness expresses

275

the absurd attachment of the poet to a fantastic and musical womb, a hollow wherein he might wish to hide his mysterious and secret origin.

WHAT SILK EMBALMED BY TIME

Every reader of Mallarmé knows how large a part is played in his work by the evocation of a woman's hair (always blonde, by the way, in contrast to Baudelaire): a flow of precious metal in *Hérodiade*, the 'considerable tuft' becomes elsewhere golden sunlight, a jet of flame, here a flag. This last metaphor is the most original. It was suggested by a spectacle which, at least about 1900, was quite commonplace: a woman before her mirror drawing with her comb the tresses 'out of the mirror' as it seems to the onlooker, like a silk banner of which her body is the standard. It was apparently a day of national rejoicing with innumerable flags flying in the street and waving slowly ('meditating'), and from this conjunction arose in Mallarmé's mind the comparison which is the subject of the poem.

The first quatrain outlines the idea: what flag ('silk') however magnificent and glorious, were it for instance one of those ancient Chinese banners whose silk, softened ('embalmed') [41] by time, displays some dragon

[41] The same image occurs in *Remémoration d'amis Belges* (see pages 145 and 216):

with tenuous coils and worn-out colour (the two senses of 'extenuated'), what flag can compare with this 'light and silken cloud that you seem to draw out of your mirror?' 'Native' is a word which often recurs in Mallarmé when speaking of female nudity.

> 'Towards which natively woman unveils,'
> (*Herodias.*)

The second quatrain develops the antithesis: what glory compares with love? To the triumph of the streets Mallarmé opposes secret tendernesses. The word 'holes' is full of difficulty. Two possibilities suggest themselves: (1) 'The holes of meditating flags' may mean the spaces between the flags as they wave together, or (2) bullet-holes in the flags, which in that case would either be historical flags brought out for a special occasion, or perhaps torn banners carved on a military monument.

Forgetting the triumphs outside, the lover buries his face in the beloved's hair. He bites it and seems to choke in it a cry. Is not this the cry of glory which he has renounced? For glory demands a cry of triumph — the soldiers carved on triumphal arches under their ragged banners open wide their mouths of stone. To prefer to such public acclamations the sweetnesses of private love implies choking the cry of possible glories in an amorous encounter. This renunciation is a gift, an

---

'Sinon d'épandre pour baume antique le temps.'
('If not to pour time for an ancient balm.')

offering to his love, a 'diamond' which he places in her hair — an ideal diamond no doubt, but none the less princely.

TO GET MYSELF INTO YOUR STORY

It would be absurd to see nothing in Mallarmé's poems but obscenities more or less veiled. It has been done, and with a stupidity that can astound the most experienced. On the other hand, it would be just as extreme not to see the rôle played by erotic feeling untinged by morbidity. The *Après-Midi d'un Faune*, in spite of the symbolism with which one may clothe it, remains all the same that of a real faun whose gestures and desires ingenuously ignore Christian prohibitions. And Mallarmé's audacity in this direction could go to real crudity, as in the poem *Une Négresse par le démon secouée*. After all, this is as ancient as literary tradition, and even the austere Malherbe advised his pupils to practise erotic compositions.

It is useless then in such poems to balk the amorous implications they suggest so insistently. Of course 'M'introduire dans ton histoire' means, to take a place in your existence, but the nature of this intrusion is not left in doubt.[42] Only thus can we explain the words

[42] In colloquial French *histoire* is much vaguer than 'story' and can mean any sort of object.

'glaciers,' 'péché' (to say nothing of 'gazon'), and the ironic triumph of the end.

Nothing Mallarmé has written is more Chinese than the ceremonious reticent irony with which he treats this misadventure. No doubt the poet had his success, but the beloved proved cold, alas: 'Violator of glaciers,' the conqueror never lost the feeling that he had out-stepped the permissible limits, that he had unduly crossed a sacred frontier and trodden forbidden ground. Hence his comic anxiety ('hero affrighted'). He felt that it was as a thief that he obtained his place in her ex-istence. The grammar itself retains something of this reticence. I see a suppressed query: 'To get myself into your story?' Yes, but only as a frightened hero.

The second quatrain explains this lack of abandon-ment, these polite protestations: the beloved was so cold that she always froze on the ingenuous culprit's lips the laugh of triumph. (In the translation 'laughing's' is a contraction of 'laughing its.')

The poet then has not tasted all the fruits of his victory. Very well then, since no triumph is conceded, he will command one for himself, as poets can at the expense of their imagination. And it shall be a real triumph in the antique style, with a chariot, imperial purple, and scattered kingdoms all around.

What actual situation served as a point of departure for this grandiose illusion? Was it, as M. Paul Valéry suggested, a promenade in a carriage with wheels either actually red or merely reddened by the reflection of a setting sun? It is natural to imagine the two lovers going for a drive and Mallarmé thinking, with a smile, 'at last here is my triumph' whilst looking at the wheels which turn purple in the air pierced by the rays of the setting sun. The realms are evidently in the cloud-landscape.[43] 'Thunder' in this at once suggests the thundering of a chariot and the explosion of his joy.

A possible alternative explanation occurs: if one imagines that the lovers go to a show of fireworks, the wheel becomes a set-piece with red lights and explosions at the centre, dying to purple on the circumference.

But these hypotheses are unimportant. Whatever the actual facts may have been, he chose from them only what emphasized the idea of his triumphal chariot. The word 'sole' in the last line is the only one which refers to the quatrains by its ironic accent. After all, one only has the triumphs that one can.

TO THE OVERWHELMING BLACKNESS HUSHT

The point of departure here is the spectacle of the sea in stormy weather. The water is covered with a network of foam under heavy clouds. Mallarmé has the impres-

---

[43] Cf. in *Another Fan*:
    'The sceptre of rose-red shores
    Stagnant on evenings of gold . . .'

sion that something has happened. What? He makes two suppositions, (1) in the octet: perhaps a ship has been swallowed up without a sound ('husht'), its hooter useless ('virtueless'), sail stripped from the mast; (2) the other in the sextet: perhaps the abyss, furious at not having brought about a grand shipwreck ('some high perdition') and at having used all its force in vain, may have in its 'niggard wise' drowned the flank of a siren child, in the white line of foam left by the undertow.

The construction in French is difficult. One may perhaps reconstruct it prosaically thus:

Quel sépulcral naufrage — tu (*unsaid* [44]) à même les échos esclaves par une trompe sans vertu à la nue accablante basse de basalte et de laves,[45] — quel sépulcral naufrage (tu le sais, écume, mais y baves) abolit le mât dévêtu, une (épave) suprême entre les épaves —
Ou (bien est ce) cela que, etc.

The fundamental construction, with an assured poetic logic, gives an impression of silence and overwhelming disaster, an impression preceding any explanation.

The 'so-white dragging hair' is clearly the line of foam left by a retreating wave.

[44] Unsaid, by the trump, to the blackness . . .
[45] Cf. *Tombeau* (*de Verlaine*) — 'The black rock . . .'

MY OLD BOOKS CLOSED ON PAPHOS' NAME

This is a simple account of a reverie at a period when everything brought Mallarmé back to his obsessions — the supremacy of the imaginary over the real, of the possible over that which has been, of absence over presence. By living so constantly on the confines of the ideal and actual, as it were on the borders of nothingness, by constantly relating the non-existent to the existent by metaphors, and by modulating from words to silence, as a musician between two different keys, Mallarmé came at last to prefer silence, non-existence and the ideal. He said at the beginning of his lecture on Villiers de l'Isle-Adam, 'A man accustomed to dreams comes here to speak of another who is dead.' For the dream, the ideal, and death are by now joined in his thought. These comprise the non-existent and at the same time give us the only antidote to the ennui caused by what exists too positively — 'The ennui,' he says in his *La Musique et les Lettres*, 'one feels regarding this too solid and heavy world.'

This is indeed the subject of the poem. Of two landscapes, one imaginary and the other real, he 'elects' the former; as between two breasts, one 'bursting with perfumed human flesh,' the other absent, the 'seared breast of an antique Amazon,' he chooses the second for his 'ecstatic' contemplation.

The reverie takes place, of course, by Mallarmé's fireside,[46] and is suggested by the word Paphos, whereon he closes his book. The poet evokes with his genius the splendour of a Greek temple by the sea-shore. Outside meanwhile a glacial cold reigns — very well, let it freeze in reality ('Let the cold course'), I will not lament (*nénie*, 'wail' — the Greek word for a religious lamentation is chosen for its local colour) if the snow which the wind flurries ('this so white gambol along the ground') seems to deny to any real site the possible honour of resembling his evocation ('unreal landscape').

At the end of the first tercet 'one' refers evidently to 'fruits'; then 'human' converts this fruit into a breast ready to be compared to 'the other' at the end of the second tercet.

It is not, of course, by chance that Mallarmé closes his selection of poems with this reverie concentrated on the 'other' reality.

UN COUP DE DÉS

The reader who looks at this poem for the first time will be astonished by the extraordinary typographical arrangement. The idea is however simple enough. Mallarmé wished to give visual expression to a complicated train of thought by showing us, one after another, the

[46] Once more 'Méditatif — il est (tisonne-t-on) . . .' — (*Divagations.*)

images of a kind of intellectual film. Begin by imagining a single sentence cut into fragments. The first fragment is cast upon a screen in large letters, stops a moment, then disappears. The second fragment follows in its turn and in the same print: but its appearance produces in the mind — that is to say on the screen — a secondary idea which is set down alongside the main theme. Then, once more, everything vanishes. But a new page appears and this time it is several themes, several thoughts, which are projected almost simultaneously upon the page. Then a kind of mental counterpoint begins to develop, in which, from time to time, another fragment of the main sentence appears amidst the incidents, suppositions and insinuations. And, when the last word of the main sentence is written, the secondary themes to which it has given birth die away and the poem is finished.

The unit of the poem is therefore the page and not, as in other poems, the line. There are, I repeat, many themes on each page, each in its own type and they should be read one after another, from left to right and from top to bottom (as one instinctively does). But, this having been done, every page should be considered in its entirety, as though it were a picture. It has its own composition and the manner in which the words are arranged, their proximity or distance from the principal theme, has an intellectual significance.

The creation of this new poetic form was in itself

a work of genius. Nevertheless Mallarmé has had few imitators. This is because, apart from its singular construction, the *Coup de Dés* presents three kinds of difficulty: 1) The philosophic meaning; 2) The poetical symbolism; 3) The grammatical construction. Without attempting a complete analysis I would like to help the reader to overcome these three obstacles.

．．．

The *Coup de Dés* was written in 1898; the main ideas had already been expressed in *Igitur* in 1869. Let us begin by defining the essential terms. 'Coup de Dés' means: thought. The poem makes this clear: 'Toute pensée émet un coup de dés.' Now for the word 'hasard'; it retains the meaning which it had in *Igitur*: the incidence of life and death in time ('le déroulement dans le temps des fluctations de la vie et de la mort'). The waves of the sea are a natural symbol thereof. Bear in mind that in the game, as thus conceived, death always wins in the end. As a result the word 'hasard' acquires the meaning: extinction, annihilation, impersonality. Mallarmé speaks of 'la neutralité identique du gouffre' — the indifferent neutrality of the abyss, into which everything falls. The waves rise only to fall again and in truth nothing has happened. What then becomes of the principal theme of the poem? '*Un coup de dés jamais n'abolira le hasard*' may be translated as: A thought will never conquer non-existence (or, as one may say, death). This affirmation is made without the arguments on which it is based; but they are easily to be found in the deductions of *Igitur*. What thought could overcome death save absolute thought? Now absolute thought, resulting from chance, can only be chance becoming conscious of itself, of its idea, its law, its entirety, that is to say, of its nothingness. So far from overcoming chance, absolute thought returns and identifies itself therewith. And since a relative thought could not do more than an absolute thought, a thought will never abolish chance. Q.E.D.

·   ·   ·

The title of the *Coup de Dés* is reproduced in the text in the form of a backbone. In between the words of this principal theme there are three headings: *Un coup de dés jamais* (heading A), *n'abolira* (heading B) and *le hasard* (heading C). Let us take them one by one.

Heading A. A *shipwreck*. In the storm on the sea of chance the master might throw a roll of the dice such as would give him power over the waters. He hesitates; a wave carries him away. His fist, still closed over the unthrown number, rises for an instant above the seas, leaving that supreme knowledge to a possible inheritor.

Heading B. *Hamlet*. Above the trough in the waves which follows the sinking ship a whirlwind of horror and mirth — 'tourbillon d'hilarité et d'horreur' catches the spindrift. The tallest feathers of spray become plumes in the turban of an apparition. Laughter, horror, and irony take shape. Jesting Hamlet points out that if the throw gripped by the jealous old master were indeed the Number of Numbers — absolute thought — it was none the less a chance — *le hasard*.

Heading C. *The abyss and the stars.* Only the lapping of waves troubles the surface of the abyss. Nothing has happened after all, and the result would have been just the same if the absolute thought had been born. Nevertheless, over the abyss, a constellation shines which is, perhaps, reckoning some final calculation — 'un compte total en formation.'

· · ·

In his preface to the *Coup de Dés* Mallarmé says, without further elucidation, that the poem, besides its main subject, has secondary and adjacent themes 'outre un motif prépondérant, un secondaire et d'adjacents.' There is no doubt about the principal theme. The secondary theme is, I think, that written in capital italics next largest to the capitals of the principal theme. The main and secondary themes having the same ending make a kind of fork, like two rivers flowing to the same mouth.

'Si c'était le Nombre ce serait

LE HASARD'
'UN COUP DE DÉS JAMAIS N'ABOLIRA'

Thanks to a generous use of very loose grammatical ties — apposition, subordinate clauses, parentheses — the adjacent themes are so freely arranged as to be almost detached. In this way the pages form a kind of picture. If they were printed on a scroll they could be unrolled upon the wall like a Chinese painting.

AN EARLY INTRODUCTION BY ROGER FRY

MALLARMÉ is reported to have said that he was the first pure poet. If we put it that he was the first poet to aim consciously and deliberately at purity we shall perhaps get a useful clue to understanding his poetry.

Almost all works of art are more or less impure; that is to say, they allow or even excite in the contemplator echoes of the emotions which are aroused by actual life, such as pity, fear, desire, curiosity. So that our reaction to such works is (at all events for a time) compounded of certain emotional states which are connected with life, together with those purely detached emotions which are peculiar to esthetic apprehension.

I wish to leave aside for the present the question of whether purity is desirable or not in a work of art, and will merely constate that in proportion as he becomes more conscious of his purpose the artist tends towards purity — tends to concentrate his attention and his powers on the detached esthetic emotions.

Mallarmé then may be an interesting case for esthetic theory, since we may distinguish more easily in his work than elsewhere the nature of pure poetic form. Our search must be for the fundamental necessary quality of poetry, for that without which a work cannot be said to be a poem. I scarcely hope to discover this completely, I only hope to disentangle certain elements and put them in a clearer light.

Every word carries with it an image or an idea surrounded by a vague aura of associations. This aura no doubt will vary as it were in shape and colour for every single individual, but for those who are familiar with a language there will be a general and substantial resemblance.

When a word is apprehended, then, this aura takes shape in the mind, and when a second word is joined to the first (as for instance in apposition, or as an adjective to a noun) this changes the aura of the first word, expanding, contracting or colouring it as the case may be, and the resultant complex will again suffer a change as its relation with the total complex of the statement is made evident by the syntactical construction.

The purpose and nature of a sentence such as I have just written is to give as little emphasis as possible to the associations or auras of the words used. The result aimed at has been purely intellectual exposition and not esthetic pleasure. The essence of poetry, on the other hand, seems to be to use words in such a way that they attain the maximum of evocative energy. The poet so arranges that each word shall have as full, as rich, as completely visible an aura as possible, and that the changes which each word makes in the aural complex shall have such a rhythm that as we proceed each change tends to become more and more significant.

If we think of any moving phrase in the climax of a great drama we shall see that its impressiveness is due to the accumulation in the mind of such a complex. When King Lear says:

> 'Didst thou give all to thy two daughters,
> And art thou come to this?' [1]

the word 'daughter' has at this point in the play acquired a quite peculiar potency. In a thousand other contexts the same word might be entirely trivial.

It has often been noted that a certain quality of surprise, or at least unexpectedness, is essential to keep our contemplation at full stretch, but this surprise must be as continually resolved and harmonised with the total aural complex.

A word may make a sudden change, but the change must be rhythmically related to the sequence of preceding changes.

As a fairly good instance of this cumulative effect of the interaction of the auras of words, I take the beginning of the Epitaph in Gray's *Elegy*:

> 'Here rests his head upon the lap of Earth
> A Youth,'

The mind has already been attuned by the preceding lines of the poem to a special emotional state about

---

[1] I have filled in the blank left by Roger Fry for a quotation to the best of my ability. There are other plausible lines in *Lear* that might be inserted, but this, to Edgar on the heath, seems the best illustration for the point. — J. B.

death and the posthumous life of fame. *Here rests* [2] is of course the conventional beginning of epitaphs, and produces if anything a certain emotional dreariness.

But we are brought up sharply when instead of the customary 'the body of,' 'his head' shows us that 'rests' is used transitively. The first effect of this is a slight suspense and anticipation, since the inversion compels us to wait in order to know exactly what the subject is. The other effect is that, since we already guess that the subject is the dead person, it gives an unexpected vividness and force to the image of the action.

Upon the lap defines and greatly heightens the effect of the gesture already visualised in the mind, and the whole complex is intensified and completed by the word *earth* with its implied personification and suggestion therewith of compassionate sympathy. Finally, *a youth* gives at once the touch of universality and undistinction as well as pathos, which is in key with the whole preceding poem.

It will be recognised that such a method of bringing out the full significance of word images by their relative positions as is here analysed belongs also to wit, and indeed wit and this quality of poetry are very nearly allied.

When Mallarmé's *Hérodiade* says:

[2] Roger Fry failed to make the (not very important) change needed in his comments after verifying his quotation and replacing 'Here rests' by the correct 'he rests.'

> 'O femme, un baiser me tûrait
> Si la beauté n'était la mort,'

we recognise that with a different intention such a phrase would become witty (*e.g.* capax imperii nisi imperasset).[3]

It is indeed by playing upon this similarity of form that parody gets its easiest effects, since it is only necessary to keep the form and alter the intention in an opposite direction.

Of language arranged in verse form, at least half, if one considers the mass of comic journals, has a witty rather than a poetical purpose. So that the association of poetry with the verse form, though generally true, is only half the truth, and the use of poetry as nearly conterminous with verse is misleading, even if we include bad poetry.

Both poetry and wit employ the verse form for the same reason, namely, that it increases the power of heightening the effect of verbal images by emphasising their interrelations. Rhyme also has particularly the power of arousing anticipation and surprised acquiescence, or it may be, in the case of wit, unresolved shock.

In the sentence already quoted from Mallarmé, the break of the verse at 'tûrait' not only intensifies the violence of this word, but heightens the effect of the

[3] Roger Fry also gives as an example, on the back of a rough draft:

> 'Ope thy mouth to its uttermost measure
> And bite us again. . . .' — J. B.

descent on the conditional clause. Had the intention been witty, the break would have had a precisely similar purpose and value.

I suggest tentatively that the distinction between poetical and witty effects of language may be that in poetry the complex of word images and their associations tend to set up vibrations which continue in the mind, whereas wit brings the vibrations to a more or less sudden stop.

For instance, the Chinese 'Stop-short' is defined as the opposite of an epigram in that the words stop short, but the sense goes on.

It is evident that in witty verse any arresting melody of sound would be misplaced, since it would tend to arouse a mental state conflicting with the effect of the word-image complex. But where verse is employed for poetical ends, beauty of sound may not only not be impertinent, but may greatly heighten the effect of the words by producing a rich vague emotional state in harmony with the expression.[4]

Herein lies one of the crucial questions of any possible esthetic of poetry, for so great is the importance of this melodic effect that it frequently appears to be the most essential and fundamental characteristic of poetry.

Three possible explanations suggest themselves:

(1) The word image-complex, which I have tried to

[4] The rough draft reads: 'a mental tune exactly fitted for the effect.'

describe above, is the fundamental quality of poetry, and melody is ancillary to that, being, as it were, a physiological aid to poetic apprehension. If this is so, Goethe was right when he said that the fundamental quality of poetry was capable of translation into another language.

(2) The melody is the essential effect of poetry, and the verbal images merely, as it were, form a channel for the flow of the vague emotion aroused by the melody.

(3) Both of these two things enter, as it were, into chemical combination. They are inseparable, and together make the single fundamental essence of poetry.

That the second hypothesis is wrong seems to me fairly evident. One must not, in order to test this, take Lear's nonsense verses, since these are no mere verbal melody; they have sequences of verbal images which for all their vagueness react upon one another precisely as in ordinary poetry. We must consider rather what esthetic emotion is aroused in us when we listen to poetry recited to us in a completely unknown language. We then have the melody, pure and simple, and its effect seems to me very slight indeed. Its effect is incomparably feebler than that of music, and scarcely calls for canalisation, such as I take to be the main effect of words in a song.

It is much more difficult to dispose of the third hypothesis, but I doubt the possibility of this complete identification of the two effects.

One reason which makes me doubt whether complete combination takes place is that the melody taken by itself is more monotonous, has a lesser range of variation, than the verbal image of sequence. Another reason is that what appear to me to be purely and completely poetical effects are sometimes found in prose writing, and that not in prose where the melodic effect resembles that of poetry, as for instance in parts of the Bible, but in prose that has no strongly marked melodic effect at all. While admitting, therefore, the singular appropriateness of melodic rhythm to poetic effect, and its marked power of heightening the effect of the word-image sequence, I still incline to think that sequence of word-images and their auras is the most fundamental quality of poetry.

It is seen, then, to be essential to the poetic effect that the meaning of the words in the fullest sense, and including all their overtones of feeling, should be peculiarly evident. Nevertheless, the meaning of the phrase in the sense of its truth to fact, its value for life, its importance, its interest, does not enter into consideration. It is, for instance, quite irrelevant to the consideration of Dante's poetry that he presents a universe which contradicts flatly our own experience of the nature of things. Such meaning, then, as can be conveyed as well, or better, by quite other words, in a paraphrase, is not part of the poetical effect.

[⁵ If I am right, this beauty of sound is rather a favourable accompaniment than part of the essential quality. It may almost be described as a physiological aid to esthetic perception. If this is so, Goethe was right when he said that the essence of a poem was capable of translation. But though the meaning of the words and phrases is thus seen to be essential to the poetic effect, the nature of the meaning, its truth to fact, its value for life, its importance, its interest, do not enter into consideration. Such meaning as may be conveyed as well or better in a paraphrase is not part of the poetical effect. Any meaning in this sense, any content that is, is theoretically capable of becoming the nucleus for the crystallisation of a poetic whole, and from the point of view of pure poetry its nature is negligible.

If I am right in thinking that this cumulative effect of the auras of words is the essential quality of the poetic art, Mallarmé must be regarded as one of the poets who has studied it most intently and deliberately. It may, of course, be discovered that this conscious and deliberate focussing on the essence of an art is not fortunate for the artist. It may be that the greatest art is not the purest, that the richest forms only emerge from a certain richness of content, however unimportant that content may be in the final result. But, these are questions which

⁵ The brackets mark a passage from the rough draft.

concern the psychology of artistic production, rather than the nature of esthetic perception. Certainly no poet has set words with greater art in their surroundings, or given them by their setting, a more sudden and unexpected evocative power.]

Mallarmé's preoccupation is then with the purely poetical relation of verbal images and ideas. His recognition of these relations is perfectly detached. He never takes sides: he is never tendentious. A great deal of poetry endeavours to force the poetical pitch of emotion by deliberately heightening and aggrandising the object contemplated. Such poets employ adjectives and similes which elevate the tone, and are more remarkable for their rhetorical effect than for their exact applicability:

> 'Nor dim, nor red, like God's own head,
> The glorious sun uprist.'

When this habit becomes exaggerated it produces bombast, which has been reprehended ever since Shakespeare's day. But since the romantic epoch very little poetry is entirely free from it. It happens sometimes that in a violent revulsion from this fault writers fall into the opposite error of finding relations which degrade the object, as, for instance, Mr. Joyce when he talks of 'the snot-green sea,' where it must be admitted that the adjective is exact, but is even more disagreeable than illuminating.

[[6] Mallarmé said of himself that he was the first to write 'pure poetry,' and certainly he is the 'purest' poet that we know. It is perhaps only another way of putting it to say that he is the least 'poetical' poet, or again that he is the most classical. I take at random any one of our 'poetical' poets, Mr. Lascelles Abercrombie for instance. In his *St. Thomas*, ships are described as 'lean hounds.'

Here the simile has already got its charge of emotion (heightened, of course, by the choice of language), and this is as it were imposed on the object described. It is not the result of a feeling about the object, it only creates an emotional atmosphere through which we contemplate the object. The poetical poet makes use of words and material already consecrated by poetry, and with this he ornaments and embroiders his own theme. Mallarmé's method is the opposite of this. His poetry is the unfolding of something implicit in the theme. By the contemplation of the theme he discovers new and unsuspected relations. He is not concerned that the theme itself, or the objects it comprises, should already have poetical quality, nor does he seek to find relations with other things already charged with emotion.] Mallarmé is in this respect [7] singularly free from bias. His attitude is purely detached and objective and, as is natural to so pure a poet, the emotional quality of the

[6] The brackets mark a passage from the rough draft.

[7] 'This respect' is the choice of elevated or degrading comparisons. — J. B.

heme is of no consequence to him so long as it provokes
in him the impassioned contemplation of its poetical
relations. It is of no consequence, that is, whether the
subject is in its associations what is ordinarily called
poetical; that is to say, noble and impressive, or entirely
trivial and commonplace. Few poets have devoted so
large a portion of their œuvre to subjects which, were
it a question of painting, we should classify as still-life.
No one has given to the words for common objects so
rich a poetical vibration — fenêtre, vitre, console, verrerie, pierrerie, lampe, plafond — and this by no forced
note of admiration or willed ecstasy, but by an exact
observation and deduction of their poetical implications. Perhaps he was humorously conscious of carrying
this method to an extreme when he described a man
on a bicycle as 'one who unrolls between his legs the
image of an endless rail.' But in this caricature we can
see the essential quality of his method.

This desire to exhaust even in the most trivial themes
the possible poetical relations, explains at once Mallarmé's syntax and his so often resulting obscurity. For
him it was essential to bring out all the cross-correspond-
ences and interpenetrations of the verbal images. To do
this it is often necessary to bring words into closer opposition than an ordinary statement would allow, or it
may be necessary that a particular word should continue
to vibrate as it were for a long time, until its vibration can
be taken up by another word. Of course, in almost all

poetry the need for this is more or less apparent, with corresponding inversions and distortions of ordinary diction, but in Mallarmé it goes to extreme lengths, and frequently causes the reader some laborious intellectual straphanging. In fact, with Mallarmé the theme is frequently as it were broken to pieces in the process of poetical analysis, and is reconstructed, not according to the relations of experience but of pure poetical necessity. In this he anticipated by many years the methods of some Cubist painters.

In this method Mallarmé makes an extreme use of the possibilities of French grammatical construction, relying particularly on genders to re-establish the suspended connections between his word-images. This naturally occasions a great and sometimes insurmountable difficulty in translation owing to the more analytical nature of the English language. I have thought it desirable in this attempted translation of certain poems to add explanatory notes, and these will, I hope, make clear the essentials of Mallarmé's poetic method. But I have confined my explanations to the first literal sense of the poems, leaving to the reader the task of following out according to his own ideas the secondary and metaphorical meaning which is, I think, always present.[8] Mallarmé's poetry has, I think, to an extraordinary degree the power of starting vibrations in the mind whose

[8] This is, of course, written of the early version, before C. Mauron's commentaries had been added. — J. B.

overtones ring through planes of thought and feeling quite remote from those with which the poem is ostensibly concerned. But there is a certain danger for the critic in laying down any precise line of thought. M. Thibaudet, in his large work on Mallarmé's poetry, follows him even into the recesses of the Hegelian dialectic. I have thought it wiser to leave the direction of these flights of the contemplative mind to the reader's own discretion. The notes, therefore, must be considered as helps only to the understanding of the immediate literal interpretation of the poems. In my translation I have aimed above all at literalness with so much of a rhythmic order in the sound as would not hamper that too much. Here and there, of course, literal-exactitude has had to give way to the exigences of a rhythm already established, and in these cases the reader is warned in a note of the failure to reconcile the two elements.

Mallarmé is so difficult that anything like a perfect translation can only be accomplished by incessant revision and the assistance of many minds. Like the Bible he should be translated by a Committee. This publication may serve to enlarge the membership of the Committee — but already I owe much help to many friendly advisers, to all of whom I tender my thanks. I must acknowledge in especial the following: Miss P. Strachey (who has, I think, deciphered more of Mallarmé's riddles than any one other person); M. André Gide; M. Paul Valéry, for heading me off one or two disastrous mistranslations and for some first-hand information about Mallarmé's 'interiors'; and Mr. Eric Maclagan, who detected several howlers. Some howlers are sure to have escaped notice, so that the present issue must be regarded as only a preliminary essay towards a final translation.

OUVERTURE ANCIENNE D'HÉRODIADE

LA NOURRICE (*Incantation*)

Abolie, et son aile affreuse dans les larmes
Du bassin, aboli, qui mire les alarmes,
Des ors nus fustigeant l'espace cramoisi,
Une Aurore a, plumage héraldique, choisi
Notre tour cinéraire et sacrificatrice,
Lourde tombe qu'a fuie un bel oiseau, caprice
Solitaire d'aurore au vain plumage noir . . .
Ah! des pays déchus et tristes le manoir!
Pas de clapotement! L'eau morne se résigne,
Que ne visite plus la plume ni le cygne
Inoubliable: l'eau reflète l'abandon
De l'automne éteignant en elle son brandon:
Du cygne quand parmi le pâle mausolée
Ou la plume plongea la tête, désolée
Par le diamant pur de quelque étoile, mais
Antérieure, qui ne scintilla jamais.
Crime! bûcher! aurore ancienne! supplice!
Pourpre d'un ciel! Étang de la pourpre complice!
Et sur les incarnats, grand ouvert, ce vitrail.

La chambre singulière en un cadre, attirail
De siècle belliqueux, orfèvrerie éteinte,

A le neigeux jadis pour ancienne teinte,
Et sa tapisserie, au lustre nacré, plis
Inutiles avec les yeux ensevelis
De sibylles offrant leur ongle vieil aux Mages.
Une d'elles, avec un passé de ramages
Sur ma robe blanchie en l'ivoire fermé
Au ciel d'oiseaux parmi l'argent noir parsemé,
Semble, de vols partir costumée et fantôme,
Un arôme qui porte, ô roses! un arôme,
Loin du lit vide qu'un cierge soufflé cachait,
Un arôme d'ors froids rôdant sur le sachet,
Une touffe de fleurs parjures à la lune
(A la cire expirée encor s'effeuille l'une),
De qui le long regret et les tiges de qui
Trempent en un seul verre a l'éclat alangui . . .
Une Aurore traînait ses ailes dans les larmes!

Ombre magicienne aux symboliques charmes!
Une voix, du passé longue évocation,
Est-ce la mienne prête a l'incantation?
Encore dans les plis jaunes de la pensée
Traînant, antique, ainsi qu'une étoile encensée
Sur un confus amas d'ostensoirs refroidis,
Par les trous anciens et par les plis roidis
Percés selon le rythme et les dentelles pures
Du suaire laissant par ses belles guipures
Désespéré monter le vieil éclat voilé
S'élève: (ô quel lointain en ces appels célé!)

Le vieil éclat voilé du vermeil insolite,
De la voix languissant, nulle, sans acolyte,
Jettera-t-il son or par dernières splendeurs,
Elle, encore, l'antienne aux versets demandeurs,
A l'heure d'agonie et de luttes funèbres!
Et, force du silence et des noires ténèbres
Tout rentre également en l'ancien passé,
Fatidique, vaincu, monotone, lassé,
Comme l'eau des bassins anciens se résigne.

Elle a chanté, parfois incohérente, signe
Lamentable!
        le lit aux pages de vélin,
Tel, inutile et si claustral, n'est pas le lin!
Qui des rêves par plis n'a plus le cher grimoire,
Ni le dais sépulcral à la déserte moire,
Le parfum des cheveux endormis. L'avait-il?
Froide enfant, de garder en son plaisir subtil
Au matin grelottant de fleurs, ses promenades,
Et quand le soir méchant a coupé les grenades!
Le croissant, oui le seul est au cadran de fer
De l'horloge, pour poids suspendant Lucifer,
Toujours blesse, toujours une nouvelle heurée,
Par la clepsydre à la goutte obscure pleurée,
Que, délaissée, elle erre, et sur son ombre pas
Un ange accompagnant son indicible pas!
Il ne sait pas cela le roi qui salarie
Depuis longtemps la gorge ancienne est tarie.

Son père ne sait pas cela, ni le glacier
Farouche reflétant de ses armes l'acier,
Quand sur un tas gisant de cadavres sans coffre
Odorant de résine, énigmatique, il offre
Ses trompettes d'argent obscur aux vieux sapins!
Reviendra-t-il un jour des pays cisalpins!
Assez tôt? Car tout est présage et mauvais rêve!
A l'ongle qui parme le vitrage s'élève
Selon le souvenir des trompettes, le vieux
Ciel brûle, et change un doigt en un cierge envieux.
Et bientôt sa rougeur de triste crépuscule
Pénétrera du corps la cire qui recule!
De crépuscule, non, mais de rouge lever,
Lever du jour dernier qui vient tout achever,
Si triste se débat, que l'on ne sait plus l'heure
La rougeur de ce temps prophétique qui pleure
Sur l'enfant, exilée en son coeur précieux
Comme un cygne cachant en sa plume ses yeux,
Comme les mit le vieux cygne en sa plume, allée
De la plume détresse, en l'éternelle allée
De ses espoirs, pour voir les diamants élus
D'une étoile mourante, et qui ne brille plus.

INDEX OF TITLES & FIRST LINES (French)

Note: *The page numbers in brackets indicate commentaries.*

309

311